STORM WARRIOR

A BELIEVER'S STRATEGY *for* VICTORY

MAHESH CHAVDA & BONNIE CHAVDA

Chosen

Grand Rapids, Michigan

Published by Chosen Books
A division of Baker Publishing Group
P.O. Box 6287, Grand Rapids, MI 49516-6287
www.chosenbooks.com

Printed in the United States of America

Library of Congress Cataloging-in-Publication Data
Chavda, Mahesh, 1946–
    Storm warrior : a believer's strategy for victory / Mahesh Chavda & Bonnie Chavda.
        p.   cm.
    Includes bibliographical references.
    ISBN 978-0-8007-9439-2 (pbk.)
        1. Spiritual warfare. I. Chavda, Bonnie. II. Title.
BV4509.5.C448 2008
235'.4—dc22   2007038688

This book is dedicated to our
friend, mentor and teacher,
Derek Prince

No coward soul is mine, no trembler in the world's storm-troubled sphere:
I see Heaven's glories shine, and faith shines equal, arming me from fear.

—E. Brontë

CONTENTS

FOREWORD

One of the greatest privileges of my life is meeting amazing men and women of God as I travel around the world in ministry. Many of these encounters become lifelong friendships that develop into Kingdom partnerships. The consistent effect of each relationship is that it brings out the best in me for God, and I am stirred to seek Jesus all the more. Each one makes me richer in the things of God, and each person I meet has something unique to offer the Body of Christ.

While I appreciate each one's character and anointing, some stand out in a most remarkable way. Mahesh and Bonnie Chavda are in that class of people. Their reputation preceded them long before I was privileged to serve beside them in various conferences around the country. But in meeting them, I realized that the half had not been told me! They surpassed my expectations. While I was invited to each conference to *teach*, in my heart I came to *learn* from them.

For a book entitled *Storm Warrior* to have an eternal effect on its readers, it must have authors who know battle and, equally, the way of victory. Its contents must not be garnered out of classrooms and textbooks. Only in the trenches of warfare can such books be formed, if they are to have lasting impact.

And there is one more qualification that not every warrior in Christ has stepped into: *a view of the devil through God's eyes.* Many war-torn individuals have the scars of battle on their minds—and the result is that they have a big devil. They can convince you of his strategies and plans. They can persuade you of the seriousness of the hour—but they have no joy. While their devil is big, tragically, their God is small.

Mahesh and Bonnie Chavda are the antithesis of that kind of war-torn believer. They illustrate courage and victory everywhere they turn. Seldom do you find a couple as qualified to write a book with this theme because seldom do you find a couple who have paid the price the Chavdas have to live in the daily experience of an authentic, victorious Gospel. They inspire me. And at times they convict me. I cannot help but hunger for more of God whenever I am with them. Their hunger for God and their experience in the supernatural lifestyle are contagious.

I love this book because it reveals, instructs and inspires. To find these three elements in any book is rare. But *Storm Warrior* is jam-packed with these elements that become tools needed to equip and release victorious warriors into a battle already won. I love this book because it releases one of the most important qualities into the heart of the believer: courage! I cannot imagine anyone reading this book who does not finish it without experiencing a supernatural rise of courage within his or her heart.

I highly recommend *Storm Warrior* to you in the same spirit in which I commend to you Mahesh and Bonnie Chavda. For they are the message.

Bill Johnson, author, *When Heaven Invades Earth*;
pastor, Bethel Church, Redding, California

PREFACE

The entire Bible is the story of the contest between two opposing kingdoms. The Old Testament records the conflict between God and the natural armies of those who opposed Him. The New Testament is the story of the confrontation between God and His spiritual enemies. From the tree in the Garden to the tree of Calvary, the Bible is a book of war. Positioned between this clash of kingdoms are the people of God. From captivity to battle plans to rules of engagement, God leads His people to triumph.

The first declaration of war was made by God to Satan as Eve looked on, her lips still wet with the juice of forbidden fruit. There God confronted man and woman for their sin and Satan for his rebellion. One was destined for redemption and the other for perpetual war and ultimate defeat. God said, "I will put enmity between you and the woman, and between your seed and her Seed; He shall bruise your head, and you shall bruise His heel" (Genesis 3:15).

The destiny of each successive generation is to be redeemed and re-equipped to walk in God's restoration amid the spiritual and sometimes natural battle surrounding us.

David, the warrior king, sang, "O LORD, You are the portion of my inheritance and my cup; You maintain my lot. The lines have fallen to me in pleasant places; yes, I have a good inheritance" (Psalm 16:5–6). This *michtam* of David was written as a prophetic declaration when he was in the midst of battle for his destiny and anointing as future king. From the days of sling and flute to leading the king's army, this warrior declared, "[God] teaches my hands to make war, so that my arms can bend a bow of bronze. You have also given me the shield of Your salvation; Your right hand has held me up" (Psalm 18:34–35).

A generation ago Winston Churchill looked out across the horizon and saw a gathering storm, a mighty contest between the forces of darkness and light. It is the same contest that has come down to us, the people of God, prepared to deliver and defend a new generation of our heritage. Isaiah prophesied that "when the enemy comes in like a flood, the Spirit of the LORD will lift up a standard against him" (Isaiah 59:19). We are the new standard bearers on whom the next generation rests.

And what is the standard? It is the cross where Jesus Christ, the captain of our salvation, proclaimed His victory by crying out, "It is finished!" and routed the commanders of His spiritual enemies. At the cross He opened the way for all who follow Him to bring the captives out of bondage and take the spoils of His mission accomplished (see Ephesians 4:8). Every believer is ordained to become an effective and joyous storm warrior of the cross. Around the standard of the cross, we who believe gather in formation, receiving the commission from the ultimate Storm Warrior: "Reoccupy and conquer until I come."

Whether it be a hidden shadow lurking inside that defeats you again and again, the challenge of physical disease threatening your child, a sudden disaster that hits your resources or an assault on your reputation or relationships, God has ordained that "in all these things we are more than conquerors through Him who loved us" (Romans 8:37).

Paul's exhortation to Jesus' warriors still stands: "No one engaged in warfare entangles himself with the affairs of this life, that he may please him who enlisted him as a soldier. And also if anyone competes in athletics, he is not crowned unless he competes according to the rules" (2 Timothy 2:4–5). The art of spiritual war is of vital importance to every follower of Jesus Christ. Learning how to live in triumph, to joy in the Spirit and to rest in the balance between grace and strength is the challenge of every believer.

Our desire in *Storm Warrior* is to share the principles and testimonies of three decades of victorious living that will inspire, train, challenge and equip you to arise in the faith of Christ and push back the spiritual forces that oppose you. We have written this book for you and your family with confidence in the anointing God has reserved for you. Our prayer is that you might arise in His wisdom and enabling power to "possess the gate of [your] enemies" (Genesis 22:17) and take hold of the riches of your inheritance in Christ.

No mortal faces life without storms. Within these pages you will find the encouragement and practical guidance to become a storm warrior.

—Mahesh and Bonnie Chavda

1

ONE WORD FROM THE GLORY

Be still, and know that I am God.

Psalm 46:10

The droplets of rain pattering down on our gathering place were a welcome sound at first. This part of North Carolina had been suffering drought conditions for some time so we were glad for a little relief. Our huge tent, which had provided shelter and covering for our conferences for several years, had endured numerous showers and storms, so we were not unduly concerned as our Waves of Glory conference commenced.

Perhaps we should have been.

The storm that had started so gently suddenly broke upon us with violent force. Great gusts of wind and torrential rain set the massive steel poles of the tent structure swinging back and forth, threatening to loose them from their moorings. A number of ushers sprang from their seats and grasped the anchor poles, trying valiantly to hold them in place. Still more ushers tried to secure the walls of the tent, grabbing in vain at the heavy fabric flapping wildly around them. Rushing water powered by a flash flood swirled past our feet. We knew that the tent was on the verge of collapsing on top of us. Our conference had drawn hundreds of people, and now their lives were in danger. We had nowhere to run.

Lessons from a Bee

A little more than a day earlier, I, Mahesh, had been deep in preparation for our upcoming conference in Charlotte. Even while exercising on my treadmill I was muttering to myself in my prayer language and seeking the word of the Lord for the meetings.

"What is Your word for this conference, Lord?" I had asked this question of Him many times and had not yet gotten any direction.

It was a warm fall day and a bee buzzed in through the open door. My eyes followed its zigzagging path around the room before it alighted on the edge of the rotating belt of the treadmill.

And there it sat, riding along on the moving belt. It could have flown away at any moment, but just like the hapless coyote in a Road Runner cartoon, it continued its ride over the edge and slipped into the machinery underneath. "To bee or not to bee?" I said, waxing somewhat poetically. Assuming that was the end of the poor bee, I turned my thoughts back to my request for a word from the Lord. This time I heard a response.

Shalom, said the still, small voice.

"*Shalom* to You, too, Lord," I replied politely. "But what is Your word for this conference?"

Shalom, the word quietly came back.

"Lord," I replied, "I know You are Jewish and all that, but right now I need Your word for this conference." My attention shifted for a moment as the body of the dead bee reappeared on the other end of the treadmill in the condition one might expect: its head smashed flat against the moving belt.

"I guess it's not to bee," I concluded.

Returning once more to communing with the Lord, I suddenly noticed a flicker of motion. I watched in amazement as the bee's head popped back into shape and the creature buzzed to life! Testing its wings once or twice, it lifted off, making its way back to the sunlit yard.

"I guess it was to bee after all!" I said with delight. "I have just witnessed a small-scale resurrection!" I knew without a doubt that radiant beams of life and power coming out from the Lord of glory had hit the dead bee as I communed with the Father. It came to life before my eyes.

In the presence of that resurrection glory I asked again, "Lord, will You please give me even one word for this conference?"

Shalom was all I heard.

Since I was apparently not going to receive inspiration or Scripture for the conference, I completed my workout and returned to my office to tend to other matters.

A Thunderous Deluge

That evening the Waves of Glory conference opened as the clear day settled into a starlit night. On the second evening, however, the afternoon skies were blackening as the attendants filed into their seats for worship.

Partway into the service it became clear that this would be more than a November rain shower. The distant rumbling of thunder grew progressively louder, and the gentle sprinkles turned into a downpour. Bonnie was in the midst of giving testimony to a time the Lord had visited her on her birthday. Her story, which included hilarious personal antics, described an outpouring of the river of the Holy Spirit into a stuffy religious church setting. She moved among the first few rows of the audience describing animatedly the ways God will come into our lives to loose us from religious bondage and oppression of the enemy.

At first the wind and sudden bursts of torrential rain added drama to Bonnie's story. At one point she even laughed out loud when thunder and lightning just beyond the cloth walls seemed to accent her point. But then the storm grew in even greater fury. Fierce winds pushed heavier bands of rain into the sides of the tent. People quickly gathered their things to keep them out of the water rising under their feet. Bonnie seemed not to notice the growing danger and continued to preach in concert with the drama of the storm. I began to pray quietly for direction as the tent seemed on the verge of collapsing. The uneasy audience looked anxiously to Bonnie and me to see what they should do.

I was able to catch Bonnie's attention and stood up to speak into the microphone: "There has been a record drought in North Carolina. Tonight, I think God is blessing this place. In the natural and in the spiritual, let the rain of the Holy Spirit come. He has said through the prophet Joel, 'I will pour out my Spirit upon all flesh and your sons and your daughters shall prophesy.' So we thank You, Father!" The congregation replied with praise and some weak clapping. And the storm bore down.

With nowhere to run and nothing but thrashing canvas between the congregation and the storm, I searched for direction and wisdom in the face of pending disaster. In the midst of chaos, from the waves of the glory that had surrounded me the previous day on the treadmill, there came a word.

In an instant I understood and said, "*Shalom.*"

At that moment, before hundreds of witnesses, the storm was completely stilled.

As soon as the word left my lips—not in ten seconds or twenty seconds or a minute, but at that instant—the raging storm ceased over the whole region. No more wind, no more rain. One word from the glory and God's perfect *shalom* ruled over the natural elements. The same glory that surrounded me as I communed with God, the same glory that resurrected the little bee, was present to calm the storm.

A shout of amazed relief and praise for deliverance went up to God. The congregation joined Bonnie and me in singing the words from a song given by the Spirit when the *shekinah* cloud of God's glory manifested during a healing service:

> Now the Lord is the Spirit, and
> Where the Spirit of the Lord is,
> There is Liberty, Liberty, Liberty.

The Testimony of the Kingdom

The morning after the storm assailed us, newscasters reported it as the worst the region had experienced in seventy years. The storm's path of destruction covered a hundred miles, and it had spawned multiple tornadoes. Our tent was at its epicenter. Yet the entire system had been stilled instantly by one word from the glory.

This is the testimony of Christ's Kingdom in the face of the winds and waves of this age: "Peace! Be still." The Father's presence is made manifest in His power to calm every storm that may arise in life—be it calamity, disease or even death. The confirmation that Jesus gave as proof of this message was the miracles He worked. Those early works were not simply enactments of social justice or even human kindness and benevolence. They were miracles attesting to a Kingdom.

God wants to make every believer an emissary of this liberty and *shalom*. We can speak it. We can carry it. We do not have to scream. We do not have to shout. We can speak to people's hearts. We can speak to principalities and powers in places of spiritual dominion. We can speak to the natural elements under their sway. We can speak to our households. We can speak to our friends and our neighbors. Our message in the storm is: "Peace! Be still."

You may ask, "How do I flow in this kind of anointing? How do I do the works of Jesus in signs and wonders?" There are two elements for receiving and walking in the miracle power of God. The first is impartation. The second is action.

It Begins with Impartation

The anointing for miracles comes through impartation of the Spirit. Moses laid hands on Joshua. Elijah laid hands on Elisha. Paul laid hands on Timothy. Jesus gives His Spirit to all who receive Him. In all of these instances the one on whom the impartation came made himself a lifelong servant of the anointing.

Impartation begins with relationship. Elisha did not just walk up to Elijah one day and ask for a double portion of his anointing. He died to himself and his vision the day he accepted the call to serve. He followed Elijah for years. Paul did not just meet Timothy at a conference and send him out to plant churches. He discipled Timothy extensively.

Receiving an impartation and transferring the anointing begins and ends as we make ourselves servants. Elisha received an impartation from Elijah. Years after Elisha was buried a dead man touched his bones and was resurrected (see 2 Kings 13:21)! Moses took his shoes off. Elijah purified himself in the wilderness. Saul got knocked off his donkey and his character was radically altered. Each of them communed with the Living Presence of God and went from serving his own purpose to serving God's purpose. God was investing in men who had become His "servants." In communion with Him they received the anointing they imparted to others. When Jesus was baptized He did so "to fulfill all obedience." The Holy Spirit descends and remains on those who demonstrate the Lamb.

Impartation and communion in harmony with the Father enable believers to carry miracles. As we make the decision to live as servants in communion with God, we become emissaries of His power to calm the storm. As I communed with Him that afternoon on my treadmill, the word for the miracle was imparted to my spirit. I picked up the vibration of heaven and calmed the storm with a single word from the glory.

It may have been a simple word like *shalom*. But in that one word from the glory resides the creative power of the universe. God's living word in a given situation can bring the dead back to life again. So it was when Elijah raised the Shunammite's son. Pacing back and forth before the boy's dead body, Elijah picked up the sound of heaven and became a transmitter of the life of Him who sits on the throne. By the Spirit, Elijah gathered to himself the breath of life emanating from the throne, and breathed that breath into the boy.

Receiving impartation is something like being a tuning fork. When one strikes a tuning fork it sends out waves of sound. Tuning forks with the same resonance will pick up that vibration and "sing along." In the same way, as we get into communion with God our whole being begins to harmonize with Him. We become vessels of His miracles. God strikes the chord for a miracle. We pick it up and transmit that miracle—and the lame walk, the blind see and the dead are raised.

Science is only now beginning to discuss new discoveries that illustrate the realm of miracles. Protons, neutrons and electrons, the building blocks of all matter, are made of minute elements called *quarks*. These are tiny vibrating strings of energy. According to this model, known as "string theory," all particles, whether or not they are visible to the natural eye, are made of fundamentally the same substance. A rock, a desk, a tree or the bow of a violin is distinguished only by its resonance.

Columbia University physicist Brian Greene describes it this way:

> The only difference between the particles making up you and me and the particles that transmit gravity and the other forces is the way these tiny strings vibrate. Composed of an enormous number of these oscillating strings, the universe can be thought of as a grand cosmic symphony.[1]

Hebrews 11:3 tells us: "We understand that the worlds were framed by the word of God, so that the things which are seen were not made of things which are visible." From His glory God reigned over the chaos and empty waste before Creation. He uttered the word of His will and delight, and all the elements of nature came together in glorious harmony. Together they formed God's song. Earth, sky, the seas and dry land were filled with His voice. We live in a universe that can be described today as the quivering, dancing echo of His first proclamation, "Let there be light."

The Holy Spirit hovers over the chaos and storms of this world, carrying the power and glory of God to bring harmony where there is discord. We can carry this glorious vibration, picking up the Father's signal coming from heaven and loosing His sound on the earth. From the very beginning God has shown the proof of His being and His power through miracles. This is the way He sent Moses. This is the way He sent Elijah and the prophets. This is the way Jesus, the Son of God, came in the flesh as a man. And we know and do testify that Jesus is alive and well on planet earth. He is still doing the same works He did before. He desires to do even greater works today through anyone who believes in Him. The key is impartation. As our relationship with God brings us into harmony with the vibration of heaven, we become enabled to transmit His healing miracles to people around us. Jesus told His disciples, "As the Father has sent Me, I also send you" (John 20:21). The greater works are waiting for you!

Daniel prophesied that as the ages draw to an end, those who know their God will do great exploits (see Daniel 11:32). The miracles of Jesus on earth testified to the Presence, personal reality and power of the Father in heaven. Signs and wonders are still the testimony of the resurrection of Jesus. He intends that the Gospel of His Kingdom be proclaimed and demonstrated with the word and works of His power for all to see and hear.

It Thrives on Action

Impartation and then action. Most of us have spent a few hours watching those wonderful old Westerns, which always culminate in a final showdown with the bad guys. Modern movie versions of this theme now take place in space or on dark city streets, but the formula is generally the same. The classic scene, though, is some dusty little town in the middle of nowhere. A guitar twangs in the background. The sun is high overhead. Main Street is all but deserted.

The villain struts out of the saloon, smug in his power to strike fear in those around him. But out of nowhere our steely-eyed hero appears, his hand poised over the handle of his six-shooter. Alone and unafraid, he faces the villain. Tension mounts and in a flash of fire and smoke, the evil one is slain. His lifeless body bears testimony to the skill and courage of our hero, who quietly mounts his steed. The overjoyed townspeople emerge from their houses and watch their liberator ride into the sunset.

That may be a well-worn movie formula but it is still a good one! Could we not use a few old-fashioned heroes in our generation? We need men and women unafraid to face down evil and willing to fight to set innocent captives free.

In the real-life frontier days of the American West there was a group known as the Texas Rangers. The Rangers were famous for their grit and courage. They tracked down and imprisoned the most dangerous criminals of their day. When the Civil War ended and Texas was gripped by lawlessness, the Rangers were called on again to restore decency, law and order.

The Rangers were concerned with results, not paperwork. An individual Ranger simply went where he was needed and worked until the job was finished. Rangers could live off the land and go days on end without sleep in pursuit of their quarry. They could hold off whole mobs or overtake and arrest killers on the open range. The Rangers also made sure they had a direct line to the big boss, or "Colonel," when they needed it.

There is a story about a particular Texas town ravaged by violence. The mayor sent a telegram pleading with the governor for a force of Rangers to address the situation. The governor agreed and the townsfolk waited anxiously for their arrival. Finally, when the expected train pulled in, the towns-people stared in dismay as only one passenger emerged, a single Ranger, Captain Bill McDonald of Company B.

The mayor broke the silence, asking, "Why did the governor only send one Ranger?"

McDonald cracked a tiny smile and is said to have answered, "You ain't got but one riot, have you?"

One riot; one Ranger. It has been the Ranger motto ever since.

Today, however, the Texas Rangers serve mostly as special investigators. Being a Ranger in the modern world means fewer showdowns with evil and a lot more bureaucracy and paperwork. Many have turned in their badges in frustration. The effectiveness of the company and the Ranger motto and message have been pretty much disabled.

Do you see the similar history in the Church of Jesus Christ? The company He called a "peculiar people" and "special treasure," a Kingdom of priests called out of darkness to do greater works than He, has mostly become a company of investigators looking into the past. Aimless philosophies, watered-down theologies and fear of being rejected by the world have all been allowed to strip the Church of her badge of authority.

Too many Christians today are happy just to research past occurrences of the Gospel. The time has come for action that accompanies this Gospel. It is time to arrest the activity of the thief, robber and destroyer of people's lives. It is time for a revival of the old wild way of the apostles and prophets who saw God, received an impartation from Him, walked in His presence and did the works they saw Him do. It's high noon on Main Street, and God is looking for a company of Rangers to receive His impartation and go into action.

All in a Day's Work

For Jesus the miracles of the Father were all in a day's work. The eighth chapter of the gospel of Matthew records just such a day. Jesus came down from the mountain where He often spent the night in prayer. The first man He met was a leper. "Lord, if You are willing, You can make me clean," the man said.

"I AM willing!" Jesus replied. The man was healed.

Next He met a centurion whose servant was dying. "I will come and heal him," Jesus said.

"Only speak a word," the soldier replied.

Jesus spoke and the servant was cured at that instant.

Going on to the sea, a great multitude followed Him. When they were out on the water Jesus could finally rest and He fell asleep. But without warning a furious storm came up on the lake. Waves swept over the boat and the disciples woke Him. "Lord, save us! We are perishing!" He got up, stretched His tired body and somewhere between a weary yawn and a reprimand for His friends' lack of faith, Jesus rebuked the storm. Instant *shalom* fell upon them and arrested the raging elements. The disciples had seen all sorts of miracles, but now they asked one another in amazement, "Who can this be, that even the winds and the sea obey Him?"

The answer is simple: Jesus was a man who knew His God. He was the old gunslinger at high noon. He was the Ranger on the open plain. He was the ultimate Storm Warrior and He was on a mission: Bring the kingdom of darkness into submission.

On the other side of the same lake two demon-possessed men who lived in the tombs of the dead confronted Him. It was about midnight by this time, and the day that began early after an all-night prayer watch had been long.

"What have we to do with You, Jesus, You Son of God?" they shouted. "Have You come here to torment us before the time?" But it was not the men who spoke; it was the demons within them. In the background a herd of pigs snuffled about. The demons heard the sound of heaven gathering against them. Like thieves caught red-handed they surrendered. "If You cast us out, permit us to go away into the herd of swine," they begged.

Jesus said one word: "Go!"

The demons left the two men and rushed into the pigs, and the whole herd stampeded down the steep bank into the lake and drowned. The pig tenders ran to town to report the story, and the reaction of the townspeople is astounding. There was no rejoicing that the possessed men were set free or that the town was no longer threatened by their violence. They did not want to know who Jesus was or why He had come to their town. "The whole city came out to meet Jesus. And when they saw Him, they begged Him to depart from their region" (Matthew 8:34).

There always have been and always will be disinterested and fearful townsfolk. There always will be some who prefer demons to deliverance. There always will be a mob that wants pigs, not God. Be sure you will meet them. Some of them will be all dressed up for church!

The old theologies that claim God has stopped doing miracles are a covert way of claiming Christ never came out of the grave after His crucifixion and burial. The rationale of these theories is that Christ is dead. In essence that means His salvation is no good either. It never went into effect. But our world is also filled with people whose lifeboats are about to capsize in this storm. Who will come and rebuke the wind and waves and rescue the perishing? There are people in every city on every continent who, like the two men in the region of the Gadarenes, have been inhabited by demonic squatters and are crying out for deliverance. Who will come and sweep their houses and set the prisoners free?

The Bible claims that Jesus is the *same* yesterday, today and forever. If He is alive, He is the same Jesus who heals the sick, casts out demons, calms the storm and raises the dead to life again. If He is the same Jesus, He will be doing the same things He has always done. Jesus was either true or a liar. He is either dead or alive. He said, "He who believes in Me, the works that I do he will do also; and greater works than these he will do, because I go to My Father" (John 14:12).

The mantle for miracles has come to us through the power of Pentecost in the outpouring of the Holy Spirit.

When it comes to miracles, believing leads to seeing. Many generations of Christians have not believed and therefore have not seen. Some have even invented libraries explaining why they do not believe in miracles and theologies explaining why they do not see miracles. But our mission, should we choose to accept it, is to preach and practice the full Gospel Jesus preached and practiced in mighty works of healing and deliverance. Our message is for those who want His miracle Presence and thirst for His full salvation.

In an age of rampant rationalism and human secularism, the world is desperate for a great revival of biblical faith. Man's knowledge and ability fail when the storms come. But the knowledge of God—the intimate, personal communion with Him—shall be a rock upon which every house can be built. And we may be sure that winds will come and rains will beat upon that house, but in the knowledge of Him that house shall stand firm. As we come to know the Father intimately, as Christ did when He walked on earth, we grow to trust Him completely. That complete trust produces faith in us, and by that faith nothing is impossible. This is the secret of the Father's love that Jesus walked in. Out of that realm of communion, the miracles of healing and deliverance came forth every day in every place He proclaimed the good news of salvation. Knowledge brings trust. Trust produces faith. Faith shows forth miracles. Know. Trust. Believe. This is the foundation of a life destined for victory. We will show you how to build on this foundation in coming chapters.

One word from the Presence is enough to quell the great storm you may be facing today. One word from the glory is more than enough to silence the fiercest wind and rising flood facing your family. We live in a period of great gathering storms. Nations need healing; men need deliverance. Violence and terrorism are on the rise. The events of 9/11 are symptoms of an outbreak of global warfare with spiritual roots and implications for us all. Natural disasters and pandemics threaten defenseless populations.

Christians must be equipped to carry God's response in the midst of these storms. Christ has awakened from the dead and is alive in us. Our response should be the same as His. What does He want us to understand? His answer, coming from the realms of glory where His miracles dwell in His presence, is simple: *"Tell My people they are storm warriors."*

2

ROW TOWARD THE WAVE!

For He commands and raises the stormy wind, which lifts
up the waves of the sea.

Psalm 107:25

Most of us remember the devastation of the "Death Wave"
that struck Southeast Asia the day after Christmas in 2004.
The tsunami, a tidal wave of enormous height triggered by
an underwater earthquake, killed more than two hundred
thousand people in a matter of minutes. Hundreds of thousands more were left homeless.

A few years earlier, the sight of a similar tsunami jolted a
sleepy New Guinea fishing village into a frenzy. Panicked, the
villagers rushed to find safety on higher ground. Everyone in
the village followed the natural instinct to flee farther inland,
away from the path of the oncoming wall of water. Everyone,
that is, except for one small group of families seen dotting the
horizon in their small fishing vessels as they rowed steadily

out to sea. Their story gives us a powerful picture of courage that every storm warrior needs in order to be more than a conqueror. It comes from relationship.

These families were a close-knit group drawn together by their faith in God—even as they were ostracized and persecuted by much of the village because of it. They met regularly for corporate prayer, and it was in this setting that the Lord warned them of an impending disaster. The group had the distinct impression that the Lord was directing them to place their families into their small fishing boats and row out to sea. *Row toward the wave!* was the word that they heard.

Used to depending on the Lord's voice for survival in the hostile spiritual climate of their village, the families did not hesitate to follow the word of instruction. As other villagers looked on curiously, these brave people heeded the prophetic impression, loaded their children into the fishing boats and began the arduous task of rowing out to sea.

Not long after they launched into the surf and made it past the breakers, the contour of the approaching wave became visible to them. They strained at the oars in what became literally an uphill battle to row into the rising swell of the tsunami.

Finally they crested the wave and dropped behind the wall of water. Moments later, with devastating force it crashed onto shore. Then as the breaking wave receded into the sea, the little boats were thrust out even farther. It took an entire day to row back to what was left of their village.

Upon returning to the shore, they beached their small boats and found that no one else in the village had escaped destruction. Only the families who had rowed toward the wave survived.

How many of us would have had the courage to row into a giant wave in response to the voice of the Lord? It was a strange instruction, but these were veterans of the faith. Their discernment of and obedience to the voice of the Lord were sharpened on a daily basis by the hostile spiritual climate in which they dwelled. Their lifestyle of pressing into God had made them conquerors so that when the storm came, they did not shrink back.

This kind of courage, which defines a storm warrior, is based on intimate knowledge of the Father. Let's see what the Bible tells us about developing this relationship.

Running into Battle

The Bible paints pictures of many great warriors. Let's start with one in particular who exemplifies this courage of running into a "storm." The three-thousand-year-old story of David and Goliath teaches us much about the courage of a storm warrior. David "hurried and ran toward the army to meet the Philistine" (1 Samuel 17:48). David was filled with passion. The insults hurled against him by the enemy were intended to intimidate. David took them as personal affronts to the character of his God whom he knew and loved.

"You come to me with a sword, with a spear, and with a javelin. But I come to you in the name of the Lord of hosts, the God of the armies of Israel, whom you have defied," shouted David (1 Samuel 17:45). He knew the God of Israel was Captain of the Armies. Through the years of communing with his Father in the long watches of the night defending his flocks, David grew strong in his relationship of trust and faith. The battles he fought against wolf and lion prepared him to run against a troop of giants!

I, Mahesh, lost my own father when I was five years old. But my heavenly Father came and took me up, gave me His name and propelled me toward a destiny fuller than anything my earthly father could have dreamed of. "When my father and my mother forsake me, then the LORD will take care of me" (Psalm 27:10). David's father, Jesse, did not see David as the heir apparent to Israel's throne. But the God of heaven in whom David the shepherd boy trusted had an eye on this son of the Kingdom. God had determined to make David great through intimate knowledge of his heavenly Father.

We began this book on this foundation: Know. Trust. Believe. These first steps position us for intimate communion in an ongoing relationship with God. We draw strength to overcome out of that relationship. The challenges we face bring us into victory. But we can move beyond victory to triumph. Our first son, Ben, was born with life-threatening problems stemming from a congenital birth defect. He had a 3 percent chance for survival and normalcy. He was, in fact, expected to die of kidney failure just days after his birth. When we were told Ben would not survive the night we got on our knees and laid down our lives before God. "We will still serve You with all our hearts no matter what," we prayed. Then we got up and went to war in the Spirit with the help of our church family.

Victory did not come overnight. It was won with many prayers, much fasting and lots of tears. The strategies we learned from that battle gave us strength for the war we faced when our next son, Aaron, was conceived. Aaron had fewer than zero statistics in his favor. Bonnie will tell you that story in a later chapter. We moved from faith through faithfulness to victory and beyond to triumph. They are all alive and well today.

David did not just mouth the name of God. He lived in confidence and power from intimate knowledge of the One whose name he invoked.

Revelation of the Name

David is just one example of someone who grew in relationship because God had given revelation of His name. God reveals His name in order to impart living truth into the hearts of His children. "Who is this King-Glory? God, armed and battle-ready. . . . Who is this King-Glory? God-of-the-Angel-Armies: he is King-Glory" (Psalm 24:8, 10, message).

Again we see that impartation leads to action, and the foundation is relationship with the Father. After the Israelites had crossed the Red Sea out of Egypt, God promised that if they would follow His commandments they would not suffer the diseases "which I have brought on the Egyptians" (Exodus 15:26). Then He revealed Himself to them by this name: "the Lord who heals you" (verse 26).

When Abraham and his household plundered the armies of four kings, rescuing his nephew Lot, God revealed Himself as "God Most High" (Genesis 14:19). Recognizing that his victory had come in this name, Abraham gave a tithe of all of the spoils to Melchizedek. Then the Lord revealed Himself to Abraham as "I am your shield, your exceedingly great reward" (Genesis 15:1).

In each of these instances, God revealed His name to His children after they had encountered and overcome a storm. The living truth imparted through the experience was transformed into a name that they could call upon with confidence because of intimate, firsthand experience with

His presence. The sacred name YHWH encompasses the eternal power and love revealed in every unveiling of the name of God. Jesus is the ultimate manifestation of this name. Jesus prayed:

> "I have manifested Your name to the men whom You have given Me out of the world. . . . I have known You; and these have known that You sent Me. And I have declared to them Your name, and will declare it, that the love with which You loved Me may be in them, and I in them."
>
> John 17:6, 25–26

There is power in His name when we approach Him in faith and expectation. Once you have developed a relationship with Him, He is always there, ready to reveal His name in every situation for victory in every battle. John 6:19 tells of a storm in which the disciples were alone, struggling in the wind and waves on the sea. In the fourth watch of the night Jesus came to them, walking on the water. It was an unusual sight, even for men who were used to seeing God do unusual things, and they were afraid. But once Jesus revealed Himself, they "willingly received Him into the boat, and immediately the boat was at the land where they were going" (verse 21).

When we are willing to yield to His Presence in the midst of any storm He will suddenly come to us in unusual ways. We may have struggled "all night" and now find ourselves weary with no sunrise in sight. Jesus is the same yesterday, today and forever. Wait for His appearing—perhaps He is already there but you have not recognized Him in the situation. Look again. When He steps into the boat you will find yourself suddenly on the other side of the storm. God is searching for storm warriors who are tuned to His frequency. He longs for those who desire relationship with Him such that He can reveal His name in the midst of the storms of our generation.

The key to developing that kind of relationship is an intimate knowledge of our Father—His character, His voice and His love—revealed in His name. Obedience to the name allows the attributes to be made manifest even when destruction threatens. Jesus came to reveal the Father. We are called to do the same.

Conquering through the Father's Love

In His last moments with His disciples before His death and resurrection, Jesus warned them of the coming storms: "These things I have spoken to you, that in Me you may have peace. In the world you will have tribulation; but be of good cheer, I have overcome the world" (John 16:33). This is the foundation from which Paul was able to write Romans 8:37: "In all these things we are more than conquerors through Him who loved us."

God sent His Son in order to reveal the triumph that we have in Him. Our heavenly Father is not interested in our getting just a small victory here and there; He wants us to go beyond. It is not just victory but triumph. In victory you beat your enemy. In triumph you overcome the enemy, take his possessions—his cattle, his wealth, his property—and lead him away as prisoner; you take the spoils. In the days our Bible was written, the Roman "triumph" was familiar to all. The victor in battle would march through the city streets with a train of spoils of war behind him. The procession included the gold and silver, captured enemy commanders and militia in chains, even wild animals from the region paraded in cages as subject to the conqueror. At the cross Jesus defeated principalities and powers and made this kind of spectacle of them. In His resurrection He loosed that overcoming power for all who trust Him.

Paul continues,

> For I am persuaded that neither death nor life, nor angels nor principalities nor powers, nor things present nor things to come, nor height nor depth, nor any other created thing, shall be able to separate us from the love of God which is in Christ Jesus our Lord.

> Romans 8:38–39

The cross is the ultimate expression of God's love for you. You are more than a conqueror through that love. Nothing can separate you from that love. *The Message* states it this way:

> Do you think anyone is going to be able to drive a wedge between us and Christ's love for us? . . . I'm absolutely convinced that nothing . . . absolutely *nothing* can get between us and God's love because of the way that Jesus our Master has embraced us.

> Romans 8:35, 38, emphasis added

The degree to which you walk in victory is directly related to the degree to which you develop a relationship with your heavenly Father. Without that bond you will be subject to the powers of death and destruction waging war through Satan's kingdom. His lies and oppression will threaten you at every turn. People who are living outside of an intimate relationship with the Father often think that they just need to do more warfare to experience victory in their lives. Warfare is part of the solution, but often the major issue that needs to be examined is the state of our love relationship with the heavenly Father. It is not just intellectual assent to a doctrine of truth. It is developed in the heart under the influence of the Holy Spirit. Once your relationship is secure you carry the certainty that when you ask for an egg, He will not give you a scorpion. When you need bread, He will not give you a stone.

I, Mahesh, experienced one of the most excruciatingly painful times in my life following emergency surgery during a ministry trip in England. After surgery I awoke in intensive care and discovered that the anesthesiologist had missed a large portion of my incision when he administered the epidural. Because of the sensitivity and gravity of the surgery, my body was anesthetized and restrained so that I would remain totally still during recovery. In horrible pain I was unable to alert any of the nurses to my condition. All I could do was cry out to my Father.

As soon as I said, *Father! Oh, Jesus!* the Lord was there with me. He said, *Turn around.* I could turn my head toward His voice, and there was Jesus standing in the Western Wall in Jerusalem. His hands were out and He was singing. I watched and listened as the song washed over my body. The sound of His voice was stereophonic; waves of heavenly music came from every direction surrounding me in His song of love. My pain left instantly.

It took the doctors almost 36 hours following the surgery to realize what had happened. But the song of love coming from my Father God swallowed all my pain. Soaked in His love made manifest, the natural realm bowed to victory in Jesus. As my pain was swallowed in victory I became drunk with laughter right there in intensive care! A permanent deposit of that peace and joy was made in my spirit during that visitation. My experience of God's love in the midst of the storm transformed my daily outlook from that time till this. I have more love, more compassion for others and more joy all the time than ever in my life. The song Jesus was singing to me remains in my spirit to this day and through me affects the atmosphere wherever I am. I have become a carrier of the glory I experienced.

We were designed to know and relate to our Father God. He is not content with a casual relationship. He paid the highest price to bring us into intimacy with Him and will not be satisfied with anything less. When we know Him, we walk in the faith and expectation that is in keeping with His character and love.

Our relationship with God is gauged first and foremost through the life that Jesus lived and laid down in our stead. Examining every shortcoming and failure of our lives will cause us to slip farther and farther away from the love of God. He wants us to be servants and live pure and holy lives, but this is done in the anointing. A religion of rules and regulations will not bring us into triumph. *The degree to which you will walk in victory is equal to the degree to which you will develop an intimate relationship with your loving heavenly Father.* We are conquerors because of His love. Nothing can separate us from that love. So much is available to us because of His love. God is not after a religious performance. In the open arms of Christ nailed to the tree of Calvary He draws us into full embrace. In the revelation of that love we triumph.

Secure in God's Family

Every relationship is progressive. Marriages are not the same after twenty years as they were after one year. Trust is strengthened or weakened, established or destroyed by interaction between the two partners over time. From the outset of our relationship with our heavenly Father, we access Him by faith, trusting Him at His Word. But the power of that bond is activated through our history together.

Hebrews 11:13 commends all those who "died in faith, not having received the promises, but [who] having seen them afar off were assured of them." There is a level of authority and trust that comes from firsthand encounters with our Father God. As we develop personal histories with Him, we develop deeper levels of trust born out of this experience. As we learn to trust Him, then we increase our faith.

Once we know Him we learn to trust Him. Through that faith we can rise up in the spirit of a conqueror who can move mountains. God is calling our generation to the next level beyond victory to triumph, the celebration of overcoming. Your living, breathing relationship with your Father should imitate Jesus' ultimate model.

The secret of Jesus' triumph was the certainty of God's love for Him in every situation. That certainty gave Him power for miracles. That certainty made Him know His prayers were answered. If you are feeling defeat, if you are feeling as though life has beaten you down, if you are feeling that the circumstances of your life have overwhelmed you, ask the Father to reveal His love. It will transform you. Just as the Father loves Jesus, He loves you. Jesus Himself lifted you up to be His brother or sister. You are in the family. God will be a Father to you.

When our four children were small we used to read them a book about a little bird that had temporarily lost his mommy. Everywhere he went, he asked, "Are you my mother?" He was looking for his family. "Are you my mommy? Are you my daddy?" Every person has an empty place in his heart that can only be filled by relationship with his heavenly Father. We have a generation growing up that is fatherless and motherless, but as John 1:12 tells us, "As many as received Him, to them He gave the right to become children of God." Everyone who is born again comes into the family of God.

God has designed us to live in community. We cannot have relationship with the Father in isolation. We cannot claim to know and be in relationship with the Father if we reject the rest of His children. Part of our journey is to learn about God through relationship with His family. The devil would keep you isolated. "A man who isolates himself seeks his own desire; he rages against all wise judgment" (Proverbs 18:1). We are not entities floating by ourselves, for "God sets the solitary in families" (Psalm 68:6).

If you have not found family in a local body of believers, do it today. Get plugged into the family of God under the nurture and authority of spiritual fathers and mothers appointed to watch over your soul. Part of your growth and maturity will come as you relate to and serve the family He has given you. Just as in a natural family, there are obligations with a spiritual family. You cannot come and just be a taker if you are truly in relationship in the body of Christ. Hebrews 2:10 says: "It was fitting for Him . . . in bringing many sons to glory, to make the captain of their salvation perfect through sufferings." Jesus, the firstborn of many sons, is our example of the discipline and servanthood that is the earmark of a true son.

We honor our spiritual father Derek Prince. For many years I, Mahesh, traveled with Derek as he and the members of his ministry held evangelistic meetings and trained local pastors around the globe. One day, in front of thousands of pastors at a seminar in Africa, Derek turned and said to me, "Mahesh, everything I know I've taught you, and God is going to show you more. Your ministry is going to be ten times more effective than mine because that's how the principle works."

I just cried, and Derek was crying because the anointing was so thick as he said this. This is the true heart of a father, to see his sons do greater works. This is the heart of our heavenly Father. But these works flow out of relationship with our Father in heaven and with the spiritual fathers and mothers with whom we are in practical, family relationship in our daily lives.

Today our ministry reaches hundreds of millions around the world. Many of these are in regions where Islam has ruled with an iron hand. Part of Derek's dream was to bring liberty to these captives. Through our programs in Arabic and Farsi, God is fulfilling Derek's dream through his spiritual children. We know that this is due, in part, to the impartation that was released to us as we laid aside our own agendas to serve and honor Derek in the days God gave us opportunity to be a family.

There is blessing that comes from being in a family and under authority: Impartation flows out of this alignment. A flow of spiritual authority and anointing comes down from the head to every individual who is rightly related to Christ through His body. The grace given to a spiritual father or mother is from God Himself: He multiplies blessings to us as we become working "joints" helping to build the Father's house and edify Christ's Body.

Defined by Greatness

A storm warrior defines himself by the greatness of God. You have been brought into the family of our awesome God the Father, Son and Holy Spirit, and He has already given you the victory in all things through His love. When you establish your life on this foundation, then everything else falls into place: your identity, your purpose, your destiny and your authority. As you give yourself to serve the greater vision and purpose that God has ordained for your spiritual family, you will find more and more the individual purpose and direction for your life. You have great purpose. You have great destiny because you are part of the Body of Christ.

Jesus told His disciples, "All authority has been given to Me in heaven and on earth. Go therefore" (Matthew 28:18–19). Jesus, our ultimate example of a storm warrior, shows us how to cast aside fear and doubt and row directly into the wave. Revelation of the name and love of our Father God will give us the courage to do the same.

> Blessed is the man whose strength is in You, whose heart is set on pilgrimage. As they pass through the Valley of Baca, they make it a spring; the rain also covers it with pools. They go from strength to strength; each one appears before God in Zion.
>
> Psalm 84:5–7

By following and imitating Him, we will go from strength to strength. From knowing to trusting. From believing to victory. Beyond victory to triumph.

3

ANATOMY OF A
STORM WARRIOR

And when you run, you will not stumble.

Proverbs 4:12

Some years ago I, Bonnie, was out for my daily run along a particular beach near our home at the time in Ft. Lauderdale, Florida. The weather at nine o'clock in the morning was already hot and muggy. Running was a great stress reliever for me, and that day I decided to double the distance. A tall condominium in the distance marked the "finish line."

As I warmed up and started out, these well-loved words from the opening of Hebrews 12 came to mind: "Therefore we also, since we are surrounded by so great a cloud of witnesses, let us lay aside every weight, and the sin which so easily ensnares us, and let us run with endurance the race that is set before us" (verse 1).

When I passed the halfway point I began to wonder if the goal I had set for myself was beyond my endurance. I had run mile after mile and the finish line still seemed to be a hundred miles away! I realized gradually that I was giving expression to the way I felt about life at that point. My flesh began to speak to me, echoing the weariness of my spirit: *Why are you doing this to yourself? Isn't life challenging enough? It's so hot and miserable out here. Look at all the people enjoying the ocean and relaxing. Why don't you stop now? Nobody is making you do this. Nobody is watching you run.*

It was an apt picture of how overwhelming my life felt. Mahesh and I had been through near-death experiences with our young children. We were serving as full-time pastors in our local church. Our radically different cultural backgrounds presented their own challenges in our personal lives. There were days I felt weary of it all. That morning the physical run seemed to mirror my life. I had set out with a goal, but with every step my mind was weighed down and my body protesting. The weather conditions were miserable. I was on the verge of quitting when suddenly another jogger came out of nowhere and passed me at a fast clip.

He was an older man. His head was held high and he was smiling brightly. I could see that his eyes were fixed on a distant marker, and he seemed to be telling me, *Come on. You can do it!* His demeanor—and the fact that he was probably twice my age!—sent fresh resolve through me. My body was bolstered, but the jogger affected my spirit, too. I knew I would finish the course not just that day but in my race of faith in this life as well.

All of that happened in an instant—the same instant that I recognized who the runner was. He was an elder minister and friend who had often strengthened and encouraged us.

My mind whirred. How could it be? I knew that man to be lying on his deathbed several hundred miles away!

Even as my heart formed its question, he vanished from my sight. Tears rolled down my cheeks as I received God's message from the vision: *Keep on! Run for the prize!*

I marked the time on my watch and arrived home to learn our friend had passed into glory at the very time I had seen him moving so purposefully along the beach.

The anatomy of a storm warrior is unique. These are individuals who understand faith—the faith that comes from living under Jesus' order and authority. But they are also able to go beyond faith and move into faithfulness—serving with distinction and valor to the end of their days. The Lord reminded me that day on the beach that "He is Lord of lords and King of kings; and those who are with Him are *called, chosen,* and *faithful*" (Revelation 17:14, emphasis added). I knew that my response to the call on my life would determine my being chosen for the mission God had in mind in my generation. I knew that once He had chosen and anointed me as His servant I would be required to prove myself through faithfulness day in and day out—just like putting one foot in front of the other on that beach. I knew I must reach the finish line.

The Lord Creator Father thought of you before the worlds were formed. You were in His heart, marked as His son, as His daughter, when He drew the boundaries of nations and set His creation in motion. You may remember the exact moment you first sensed God at work in your life. You may be aware of when you first recognized His voice. But even if you are still trying to figure it all out, this can be a kairos moment in your life, the time when all the conditions are right for an encounter with destiny. Jesus is saying, "This is the way. Follow Me from here!" He desires that we be sure of our calling as carriers of His presence and glory on the earth. He wants each one of us to move beyond the call into action as chosen ones. He desires for us to move beyond being chosen to prove ourselves as sons and daughters faithful to finish the race.

Adoption into God's Family

Your anatomy as a storm warrior—that is, your identity, vision, mission and authority—lies in being the child of God. Let's look at the basis for this claim:

> For ye have not received the spirit of bondage again to fear; but ye have received the Spirit of adoption, whereby we cry, Abba, Father. The Spirit itself beareth witness with our spirit, that we are the children of God: and if children, then heirs; heirs of God, and joint-heirs with Christ; if so be that we suffer with him, that we may be also glorified together.
>
> Romans 8:15–17, KJV

The cross was the battleground, the great convergence of storm systems: good and evil, flesh and spirit, law and grace. Heaven and earth met in the sinless body of the perfect Warrior Son, and He won the battle. Through faith in Jesus Christ we are no longer children of darkness. We are no longer under the authority and influence of Satan, the world, the flesh and death. The fall of our father Adam has been cut off from our spiritual DNA; we have been given a new genetic code and a new inheritance. We have been made the sons of God by the Holy Spirit of adoption! Ultimately our very bodies will be "adopted" as they are exchanged for immortality when we are transferred into eternal glory.

Sometimes an adopted son is able to recognize the value of his inheritance even more than a natural born son. As an adopted American, I, Mahesh, am daily aware of the greater advantages and blessings I possess by having been awarded the rights and privileges of citizenship in this nation. So it is with the Kingdom of God. We who were once not a people have been made the people of God.

The Holy Spirit is the "down payment," or guarantee, of our adoption. He bears witness that we are the sons of God. He testifies to our spirits in the face of the accuser when trouble comes. "Now the Lord is the Spirit; and where the Spirit of the Lord is, there is liberty" (2 Corinthians 3:17). The presence, anointing, gifts and empowerment of the Holy Spirit dwelling in us are the down payment and first fruits of our eternal inheritance.

The Hebrew word for *son* is *ben*, which means "one who builds the family name." The sons of God understand that they are builders and inheritors within the family of God, defending and building the corporate family future as well as fulfilling their personal callings. It is the opposite of the prodigal who comes and says, "Father, give me my inheritance," and then goes off to make for himself a name or ministry. Rather, it is the response of those who care less for individual fulfillment and are hungry to find how they fit into the call of the whole purpose of God manifest through His whole family. We think of the posture of Jesus lying prostrate before the Father, saying, "Father, I come as a son, not to do My will, but Yours alone." Doing the will of the Father is the heartbeat of a true son or daughter.

This sonship is exemplified by relationships within the local church body. It is through the family, both natural and spiritual, that we learn to serve and love. In this context we can be trained and positioned for effective spiritual battle. As we assume responsibility for the well-being of others and learn to serve under the authority and blessing of those God places over us we become sons in truth.

A son is not a hireling. His joy comes from building up his father's house. Let us beware of striving to be first in ministry or position ahead of someone else in a church or in the Kingdom. Let us be secure as sons and be content with obedience and perseverance for the sake of all. Let us "consider others more important than ourselves." We are seeing a new wave of glory on the horizon. It is rising over the local church. Storm warriors will be there—plugged in and prepared. As we find our places we will fulfill our destinies and build the Kingdom together. Rooted in a family we can give ourselves to build the Father's house. The result will be fruit for the hungry and leaves for healing.

Courage in Adversity

Never for me the lowered banner, never the last endeavor. . . .
A man must shape himself to a new mark directly after the old one goes to ground.

—Ernest Shackleton, Antarctic explorer

In August 1914, Ernest Shackleton set sail from London on a ship, aptly named *Endurance*, and headed across the ocean with a crew of 27 men on a quest to be the first to traverse and chart Antarctica. Their story is an epic tale of human courage, perseverance and teamwork. Brutal conditions and disastrous events plunged Shackleton and his men toward certain death again and again. It is an inspiring example of how a storm warrior gives his best for the good of all.

After just five months at sea, the explorers faced a cruel reality: Pack ice was slowly closing in on the ship. More months of brutal conditions passed, until the ship finally began breaking apart from the pressure of the ice. The men, with their sled dogs, three lifeboats and all the supplies they could carry, had to abandon their mission of exploration and apply all their energy and resources to survival. Shackleton put aside his personal vision and individual desire for exploration and embraced his new mission: the safe return of every single member of his party.

A year passed. They managed to survive on the huge "raft" of ice that supported them, but they drifted a thousand miles off course. When they were able finally to maneuver their lifeboats into the open sea they managed, miraculously, to make landfall on the edge of the Antarctic Peninsula. There they set up camp using the upturned boats for shelter. Their only food was seal meat they could catch. For fuel they rendered seal fat.

Their prospects for survival through another Antarctic winter were slim. Shackleton was faced with the choice to either wait for rescue, in hopes a whaling ship would spot them, or use what reserve and nerve they had left to attempt a risky voyage to the nearest outpost, a South Georgia station eight hundred miles away across open water. Making his decision, the captain chose who would journey with him on the rescue mission and who would stay to lead and bolster the men left behind.

With a promise to return, Shackleton and a crew of two launched back into the icy open sea. After two grueling weeks the peaks of South Georgia came into view. The whaling station was still 22 miles as the crow flies from where the men landed. Uncharted mountains and ice crevices lay between them and their destination. Shackleton wrote:

> When I look back at those days I have no doubt that Providence guided us, not only across those snow fields, but across the storm-white sea that separated Elephant Island from our landing place on South Georgia. I know that during that long and racking march of thirty-six hours over the unnamed mountains and glaciers of South Georgia it seemed to me often that we were four, not three. I said nothing to my companions on the point, but afterwards Worsely said to me, "Boss, I had a curious feeling on the march that there was another person with us."[2]

As the three men surmounted the last peak between themselves and the whaling station, they came to a giant waterfall. Knowing it could mean death at worst and shattered limbs at best, they thought of the men waiting for them and plunged into the plummeting wall of water.

Wet, frozen, tired beyond exhaustion, clothes stained and tattered, three bearded figures walked into the outskirts of Stromness whaling station. One whaler came forward, a wizened elder of the trade, and in his native Norse he said with emotion to these sailors who forged the Drake Passage and then crossed the forbidding island, "These are men."[3]

Shackleton wrote a friend that they were "mad with joy," not because they were safe but because their comrades would now be saved. An old photograph shows 22 storm warriors standing in rank along the frozen beach of Elephant

Island one hundred and five gale-swept days after landing there. Their arms raised in welcome, we know their voices were raised as well as they see their captain returning as he promised.

Standing on the bow of the rescue boat Shackleton shouted to Wild on shore, "Are you all well?"

Wild replied, "All safe, all well!"

The boss replied, "Thank God!"[4]

On the day Shackleton returned, the waiting men had only a single day's supply of food left and used the last of their fuel to set off flares that indicated their position when rescue came.

We are on an expedition of faith through the vale of this present darkness that may be fraught with dangers unforeseen. But it holds the promise of life eternal at our journey's end. When it seems we have reached the end of ourselves, our resources and every last shred of hope in our abilities or circumstances, our Captain is there by His Spirit with us and in us to guide, protect, provide and bring us through the storm.

A Heart Made Fit

Ernest Shackleton had a longing for adventure; his compassionate leadership was put to the test by giving up his own hopes and dreams. The crisis that brings out the best in persons is seldom entered into voluntarily. Esther of Bible fame is an excellent example.

Esther grew up as an orphan in a foreign land, a third-class citizen in a nation ruled by a ruthless potentate. In spite of the popularization of her story it was nothing like a romance novel. A sudden political upheaval and pending genocide opened a door for Esther to wield moral and spiritual influence she never desired. That crisis led her to gain national and historical prominence she never imagined.

The king of Persia intended to take over the world. Imagine young Esther, a virgin, faithful to God, being conscripted for her physical attributes as a concubine for a pagan king! As obedience ruled over her fears, she became an instrument of salvation for others.

Once she was in place the anointing flowed upon her in accordance with her call. God gave her favor with influential people—not the least of whom was the king. The eunuchs who had oversight of her preparation and training are types of the Holy Spirit. *Hegai* means "meditation, groaning, separation." No one had more experience in such things than a man who had been made a eunuch for purposes of stewarding another man's kingdom. Hegai was able to confirm and guide her, taken as she was from the security and identity of her family to be handed body and mind over to the king's service. *Shaasgaz* is "one who shears sheep." Often in our journey we must be willing to lose everything in order to embrace the anointing God has placed on our life. Esther's beauty treatments were an upscale boot camp of body and mind.

Sometimes we do not get a revelation of our calling until something happens that demands untapped reserves of spiritual and moral courage. Esther's character was proven in the face of trouble. Do not be surprised if trouble is the way you discover that you "have been called to the kingdom for such a time as this."

God placed His handmaiden in a position of influence. He gave her a steadfast heart and a clear head. He stripped away any personal agendas she may have had. He sent her elder advisors to steady her when she wavered. Fasting and prayer became the bridge for Esther to cross to the next level of conquest between her ability and God's intervening power. Bolstered in faith, Esther laid down her life and entrusted herself to the One who had called and chosen her. "I will go to the king, which is against the law; and if I perish, I perish!"

Esther exemplifies the character of the storm warrior. Through her willing obedience she secured the king's favor, destroyed the enemy and saved her people. We know little of her story beyond that crisis, but we do know God's people were saved through her faithfulness.

A storm warrior develops the heart to hear God's call and obey. We see Jesus going up to Jerusalem for the Passover feast knowing He has been prepared as the Lamb for all people. In Gethsemane He prays, "Not My will but Yours be done!" A storm warrior steps up to face the challenge. He is a first responder. Jesus remains faithful still.

Every Christian is called to the frontlines of the clash of kingdoms. God is not looking for talented or charismatic or even "big idea" people. He wants men and women who know Him and who will remain faithful in every season and under every circumstance. As the Victor Warrior, Jesus demonstrates these traits. Riding with Him in battle in the last days is His army of adopted sons and daughters who have developed the anatomy of storm warriors.

In Tune with the Holy Spirit

Have you ever found yourself humming the tune or singing the lyrics of a song that comes from somewhere deep inside? The melody rises and preempts any particular engagement of the mind. Gradually, you bring your whole being into harmony with the melody of the song. In a few moments you are driving along singing at the top of your lungs, transported, refreshed, rejoicing. When you arrive at your destination and step out of your car, the atmosphere that follows you fills the room and lifts the hearts of all where you are going. *The Message* translation of the Bible has this wonderful description:

> Jesus resumed talking to the people, but now tenderly. "The Father has given me all these things to do and say. This is a unique Father-Son operation, coming out of Father and Son intimacies and knowledge. No one knows the Son the way the Father does, nor the Father the way the Son does. But I'm not keeping it to myself; I'm ready to go over it line by line with anyone willing to listen. . . . Come to me. Get away with me and you'll recover your life. I'll show you how to take a real rest. Walk with me and work with me—watch how I do it. *Learn the unforced rhythms of grace.*"
>
> Matthew 11:27–29, MESSAGE, emphasis added

Storm warriors have an anatomy that harmonizes with God in any situation. We become emissaries of His healing, deliverance from bondage, and comfort and encouragement for those in despair. We pick up the vibration of His glory and route the chariots of Satan that pursue the saints of God. Our lives become His song. It is a song of love. A song of victory. A song of hope and of power. It is the song of the storm warrior, a faithful chorus of those down through the ages who know their God.

> And what more shall I say . . . [about those] who through faith conquered kingdoms, administered justice, and gained

what was promised; who shut the mouths of lions, quenched the fury of the flames, and escaped the edge of the sword; whose weakness was turned to strength; and who became powerful in battle and routed foreign armies. . . . They were stoned; they were sawed in two; they were put to death by the sword. They went about in sheepskins and goatskins, destitute, persecuted and mistreated—the world was not worthy of them. They wandered in deserts and mountains, and in caves and holes in the ground. These were all commended for their faith, yet none of them received what had been promised. God had planned something better for us so that only together with us would they be made perfect.

Hebrews 11:32–34, 37–40, NIV

The storm warrior accepts the call to subdue kingdoms, quench the violence of the sword, put enemy troops to flight and obtain an inheritance. You have been chosen to know Him and do exploits in His name. Like the most faithful Antarctic explorer of our day or the most dutiful young woman in a palace of long ago, you will find your weakness turned to strength. You will be among the called, chosen and faithful.

Storm warrior, the mission is still ahead of you. Your greatest battle awaits your willingness to move from saving faith to faithful service. All of the difficulties and storms you have encountered, all the successes that God has given you, are building the foundations in your life. Be faithful. God intends for you to have a testimony. Patience and perseverance, a good foundation, a balanced life, vital supernatural revelation and inspiration, and mundane practicality join together to make you an overcomer.

The story of Shackleton and the *Endurance* expedition serves as an example of the type of character God looks for in those He makes His sons and daughters through faith in Christ. Never after temporal glory and personal gain, the nature of a true son or daughter flows from the head down. We have an even greater Storm Warrior who has gone before us to prepare a place. He will come back for all who wait for Him.

On that last day we shall stand on these terrestrial shores, looking longingly for His appearing. And the light of His glory will thrill our hearts as He comes in the clouds. Then we shall put off this threadbare garment of our flesh for the fresh cloth of linen pure and white, the garment of mature sons. Let us endure whatever storms may come. For this purpose we have been called and chosen in Him. Let us lift up the hands that hang down. Choosing endurance, let us be found faithful, safely watching for those around us till we see our Captain returning.

4

THE STORM WARRIOR'S MISSION

And they went out and preached everywhere, the Lord working with them and confirming the word through the accompanying signs.

Mark 16:20

God has called every Christian to be salt and light in the world. Storm warriors of Jesus hold fast to this goal and stay focused on the mission of God—to proclaim Christ's Kingdom and His coming to the world around us. In other words, as we often say to ourselves, "It is not about you!" It is the big picture that gives perspective and direction through whatever challenges may come.

The apostle Paul demonstrates this storm warrior life-style. His testimony through shipwrecks and arrests and hunger and prison was not just a story of personal survival or ministry success. The Gospel was preached to sinners, miracles attested to the truth, the true spirit of prophecy rang out, lives were saved and God's mission was fully accomplished. But not because it was smooth sailing!

Let us put ourselves in Paul's shoes in just one of his many amazing stories—his journey to Rome as a prisoner, told in Acts 27. Under criminal indictment and in shackles, Paul was a passenger on a Roman freighter, headed for trial under a hostile, pagan legal system. But Paul carried the peace and authority of a free man. In that liberty he gave both comfort and strategy to those on board the ship. He did not lose sight of his goal: to preach the Gospel in Rome.

Because Paul was in tune with the Holy Spirit's frequency, he could offer prophetic insight. "Men," he said, "I perceive that this voyage will end with disaster and much loss, not only of the cargo and ship, but also our lives" (Acts 27:10). This news of potential destruction was not good. He was warning them that pushing forward would lead only to disaster. The captain and crew considered their own knowledge of the sea superior to this preacher tentmaker's viewpoint. They ignored Paul's advice and set out in a soft southerly wind.

Despite this, Paul's spirits remained high. He was on a mission and was certain that the God who had called him was faithful to complete what He had begun. We see on this and several other occasions in Paul's ministry that his lifestyle of spiritual discipline and balance not only made him a clear voice of prophetic insight but also allowed him to handle words of prophecy properly. He was secure in his relationship with the Holy Spirit and genuinely submitted to church leadership. Not dismayed or confused even when well-meaning friends who did not understand the entirety of God's plan prophesied his imprisonment, Paul had testified to the believers in Ephesus:

"I go bound in the spirit to Jerusalem, not knowing the things that will happen to me there, except that the Holy Spirit testifies in every city, saying that chains and tribulations await me. But none of these things move me; nor do I count my life dear to myself, so that I may finish my race with joy, and the ministry which I received from the Lord Jesus, to testify to the gospel of the grace of God."

Acts 20:22–24

When others interpreted the prophecies as instruction to retreat, Paul knew they were preparing him for the difficulty ahead. Now held captive on a ship heading directly into a storm, God's servant was ready. He was not bothered when the captain and crew ignored his warnings. He knew that his personal destiny extended well beyond imminent death at sea. He shifted into the role of intercessor to circumvent the plan of the enemy for their lives and his.

How different the outcome of his testimony had Paul turned inward, offended and skulking over their disdain for his wisdom and advice! Paul demonstrated the quiet confidence of one who knows that the God who gave him his mission was more than capable of sailing them through the storm. Paul knew that it was not about him! The mission was about God receiving glory and accomplishing His desire. A storm was about to threaten their lives, but he would preach the Gospel in Rome.

Lessons in the Storm

There are important lessons that we can learn from the description of the storm and the reaction of the crew, for the danger Paul had prophesied became reality. Let's look at the Scriptures that highlight the points of our study.

> But not long after, a tempestuous head wind arose, called Euroclydon. So when the ship was caught, and could not head into the wind, we let her drive. And running under the shelter of an island called Clauda, we secured the skiff with difficulty. When they had taken it on board, they used cables to undergird the ship; and fearing lest they should run aground on the Syrtis Sands, they struck sail and so were driven. And because we were exceedingly tempest-tossed, the next day they lightened the ship. On the third day we threw the ship's tackle overboard with our own hands. Now when neither sun nor stars appeared for many days, and no small tempest beat on us, all hope that we would be saved was finally given up.
>
> But after long abstinence from food, then Paul stood in the midst of them and said, "Men, you should have listened to me, and not have sailed from Crete and incurred this disaster and loss. And now I urge you to take heart, for there will be no loss of life among you, but only of the ship. For there stood by me this night an angel of the God to whom I belong and whom I serve, saying, 'Do not be afraid, Paul; you must be brought before Caesar; and indeed God has granted you all those who sail with you.' Therefore take heart, men, for I believe God that it will be just as it was told me. However, we must run aground on a certain island."
>
> Acts 27:14–26

Storms can be the vehicle God uses to reveal the hindrances and attachments that are weighing us down and preventing us from completing the mission He has planned for our lives. Storms will come. Both in the natural and the spiritual, there will be storms. They are a by-product of the clash of spiritual kingdoms that manifest in our natural circumstances every day. But the storm warrior keeps his eyes on the goal. Here are some "quick tips" in this story that help us stay focused.

1. Go with the Flow

When the tempestuous headwind arose, the little ship could not make headway. So the crew "let her drive." There will be times that you may feel as though you are being tossed about or even blown off course. Yet the response when circumstances are beyond your control might be to go with the flow.

It is better to let the storm carry you rather than wearing yourself out struggling mentally or emotionally against every new difficulty. Sometimes the devil's trick is to keep you so stirred up over the threat of opposition you wear yourself out without a fight! Paul was able to rest in the assurance that he served a heavenly Father who works all things together for his good. Before the ship was ever driven by the storm, Paul had already exhibited the peace and attitude of a storm warrior. When the captain of the ship did not heed his instruction but put out to sea, heading for certain destruction, Paul settled in for the bad weather, considering that God would get him to the destination in spite of it.

2. Give Yourself Permission to Relax

God will provide islands of refreshing in the midst of the storm that serve as an intermediate refuge. It does you no good to refuse rest because you feel either "super spiritual" or guilty! Get your mind off the battle and come back refreshed and clearheaded.

3. Let Go of All Options but God

You might find yourself seeking a dinghy to hop in and row out of difficulty. Beware of the temptation to cling to an escape backward, thinking that if you retreat the devil will leave you alone. If any "options" persuade you to abandon ship, let them go. Sometimes God's plan is simply to stay aboard, plugged into God, firmly rooted and grounded in Him. This is a time for you to become an intercessor to usher God's glory into the lives of those around you in the storm.

4. Shore Up Your Foundations

There is no substitute for your personal relationship with Jesus! There is no substitute for your personal relationship with the Holy Spirit! And there is no substitute for your personal relationship with the Bible! When the storms of life strain and stress your ship, strengthen your foundations. You can use the principles of the Word of God and the assurance of His presence to proclaim eternal truths—even when it seems that everything is falling apart around you. If you can strengthen your foundations, you will become an ark of comfort and safety for others—beginning with your family and church friends. The old story of Noah's Ark rising above the floodwaters is a type of those who have made the Most High their refuge. The Presence of His Spirit, like the *shekinah* that led Israel in a pillar of cloud and fire, becomes your strength.

5. Strike Sail

Cease to insist on personal ambition. Let go of the idea that things always need to be done your way. The breath of

God can blow you to His destination. Sometimes personal plans, prejudices, traditions, opinions or agendas act as a mighty mainsail, catching the gale force of opposing winds. Insistence on keeping those mainsails aloft in the face of a storm can bring a whole family, a whole church congregation, a whole people into ruin.

Often the best strategy when facing a seemingly insurmountable challenge is to let go and let God. When Israel was waterlogged by the influence and oppression of an army of invaders, Isaiah advised: "In returning and rest you shall be saved; in quietness and confidence shall be your strength" (Isaiah 30:15). Settling down in hope and faith in the basic promise of God's covenant with us through His Son is more than enough assurance that ultimately every enemy will be defeated. The best strategy is to "be still and know" He is God.

6. Lighten the Ship

Prioritize: Kingdom first, family second, sinners and saints third, self last. "Let us lay aside every weight, and the sin which doth so easily beset us, and let us run with patience the race that is set before us" (Hebrews 12:1, KJV). The cargo on board Paul's ship was a year's income for the shipper. Yet the extra weight when the winds arose would have meant the loss of the vessel and all aboard it.

Your weaknesses—that "extra baggage"—will come to the surface in times of opposition and difficulty. Toss that stuff overboard. Old hurts, bitterness, crippling memories and past failures should be hurled into the sea of God's forgetfulness. The things that once seemed very important in your life may be the very things you need to part with to survive a storm. The crew eventually dumped the entire load of wheat into the sea. It is not about the profit and loss sheet when lives are hanging in the balance.

7. Hold Only a Few Necessary Things

Do not wait for someone else to come along and tell you to get your act together. There are really only a few things necessary for life: food and shelter. Oftentimes depression and discouragement come from being too weighed down with the "affairs of this life." Unnecessary complications caused by too many attachments to "things"—like unproductive or expensive recreational habits—can entangle and pull you under. It is better to develop a lifestyle of contentment and simplicity now than to have to deal with a boatload of carnal preoccupations in the midst of the storm. "Having food and raiment let us be therewith content" (1 Timothy 6:8, KJV). Beware of the need to "accessorize" your life by keeping up with the Joneses. Too many possessions, like too many commitments, can cause circuit overload. You need your strength to focus on the main thing: your obedience to the call and plan of God. All those extras become unnecessary when storms threaten.

8. Hang On!

"Having done all . . . stand" (Ephesians 6:13). There will be a point where all natural and human resource and ability come to an end. At those times, however, the presence of a Spirit-filled believer is a lifeline into a different realm. Paul was that lifeline, bringing hope, encouragement and instruction from heaven that preserved the lives of all. He was a testimony to the hope that we have in every storm.

In the natural, there was no hope left for the ship and her crew. Every step that could be taken to strengthen and increase their odds of survival was overmatched by the ferocity of the storm pursuing them. The ship's captain had disregarded Paul's warning, but there was another "Captain" aboard. The Captain of these men's souls resided in Paul's heart.

Paul's lifestyle of communion and relationship with the Lord made him a voice of hope, encouragement and instruction. Our Captain wants to use us to carry His glory in just the same way.

9. Keep Your Personal Disciplines

Paul kept his faith vital. His life of discipline sharpened his spiritual discernment, and because of it he was able to give practical recommendations to the men who ran the ship. A storm warrior should be established in regular spiritual disciplines. A sudden test does not preclude them. In fact they are best developed in advance of testing. They include fasting, worship, prayer and regular fellowship with believers. Abstinence from food was one of Paul's regular spiritual disciplines; this storm did not circumvent it.

10. Give God Glory and Others Comfort

People get enough negativity. They generally are all too aware of their failures and mistakes. The true prophetic spirit is the Spirit of Christ. He was clear, full of truth and yet did not always have to be talking or even have the last word. He knew who He was and what He was destined to do.

Likewise, Paul knew when it was time to speak and when it was time to remain quiet. When he did speak, Paul said,

"Take heart." He was an emissary of grace and truth. You are anointed with the same grace to comfort, edify and encourage.

11. Realize You Are Not Alone

Paul's confidence was in the Captain who guided his life through the storm. We are never alone. The mighty Captain of angel armies is with us at all times. Angelic intervention was loosed into the situation because a storm warrior was there. In a later chapter we will look more extensively at the presence and function of God's holy angels.

12. Do Not Be Afraid

The Spirit that is in you is greater than all other power. A storm warrior carries a different spirit. "God has not given us a spirit of fear, but of power and of love and of a sound mind" (2 Timothy 1:7). When everyone else is in a panic, turning inward and intent on saving him or herself, the believer is an anchor in the storm.

13. Complete Your Mission

God had a mission for Paul. He has a mission for you and He desires that you fulfill it. Storms and circumstances will not prevent God's blessings. Jesus is looking for men and women who will be faithful to the end no matter what comes against them. As you keep your head and stay on track during a crisis, the anointing you carry will have an eternal influence on all those involved. The Presence and deliverance of God will be ushered in through your obedience and faith.

14. Stay Faithful

The storm warrior is unwavering in his faith. When the voice of the Lord came to Paul he was able to receive heavenly direction and practical wisdom. Into the fear and hopelessness, Paul gave voice to the Captain of his heart. His words and demeanor are full of the *shalom* that he carried from the day he was led on board.

A New Perspective

Imprisonment, shipwreck, possible execution—these were simply part of the passage to Paul's destiny: proclaiming the Gospel to the leader of one of the greatest empires the world has ever known. Never losing sight of the mission, and always confident in the One who had called him, Paul remained faithful in every stage of the journey.

When natural circumstances looked as if his life and mission would be dashed upon the rocky coast, Paul was a carrier of the glory that saved him and all who were with him.

> But striking a place where two seas met, they ran the ship aground; and the prow stuck fast and remained immovable, but the stern was being broken up by the violence of the waves.
>
> And the soldiers' plan was to kill the prisoners, lest any of them should swim away and escape. But the centurion, wanting to save Paul, kept them from their purpose, and commanded that those who could swim should jump overboard first and get to land, and the rest, some on boards and some on parts of the ship. And so it was that they all escaped safely to land.
>
> Acts 27:41–44

We can surmise that Satan did not want the first powerful seeds of the Gospel to be sown in Rome through Paul's testimony. We can surmise that the many threats to Paul's life were obstacles to that mission. But Paul never wavered in the word God had spoken to him. And those seeds of the Gospel, spoken by one faithful warrior, eventually uprooted the entire Roman Empire. Mission accomplished.

5

THE CALM IN THE STORM

He calms the storm, so that its waves are still. Then they are
glad because they are quiet.

Psalm 107:29–30

I, Bonnie, want to tell you in this chapter about a particularly
difficult two-year period during which Mahesh and I learned
a great deal about being storm warriors. At the time we felt
as though we were caught between powerful colliding storm
systems coming at us from every direction. Through it all,
though, we experienced the faithfulness of God. We learned
to listen to the voice of the original Storm Warrior who was
with us every step of the way. We were required ultimately
to put our lives on the line and yet He gave us the power to
overcome. We found the calm in the storm.

Heartbreak in Africa

Our saga began two decades ago deep in the bush of Zambia, Africa, where Derek Prince and Mahesh had traveled to preach the Gospel and minister miracles of healing and deliverance. After most of their luggage was stolen, they landed in Lusaka to take a single engine plane far into the interior of the Mwinilunga province. There, a large field had been cleared to accommodate the thousands of villagers who gathered daily to hear the Word of God. Morning, noon and night for more than a week, God touched these desperate and spiritually hungry people through Brother Derek and Mahesh.

God did amazing things. At one point a sixteen-year-old boy who had been crippled by polio for more than a decade suddenly straightened up and jumped out of his wheelchair! Running like a seasoned athlete, he circled the cheering, awestruck crowd. His mother came toward Mahesh, bowing and tossing handfuls of dust onto her head in her tribal custom of honoring a great chief. Weeping with joy, she exclaimed, "Thank you for coming from America and healing my son!"

Mahesh took her hands and raised her to her feet. "Mother," he said, "I am just a little servant of the greatest Chief named Jesus Christ. He is the One who healed your son today."

After an evening meeting, one of the missionary pastors asked Mahesh to visit a woman whose child was terribly ill. As he followed the pastor through the darkness to a tiny hut, Mahesh learned the woman's story. She had been married and given birth to twin boys. Her husband's tribe considered twins an evil omen so she and the boys had been sent away. While many women in such circumstances turned to prostitution to feed and clothe their children, this young woman had come to Christ shortly after and was struggling to live in faithfulness to God despite her desperate poverty.

Pushing aside the dirty cloth that served as the door of the hut, Mahesh entered and found the woman sitting on a mud floor with only the light of a single candle illuminating the darkness. In her lap she held the still body of a small boy. Near the edge of the hut was a pallet where another boy of identical appearance slept. As she handed the boy in her lap to Mahesh he immediately knew that the child had been dead for some time. His tiny body was cold and becoming stiff.

Mahesh sat down beside the woman on the mud floor and began to pray. He prayed and prayed, gently rocking the lifeless little body as the desperate mother and hopeful pastor looked on. After more than an hour Mahesh knew in his heart that there was nothing more to do. Sadly he handed the child back. The woman took him and looked up to heaven and spoke softly in her native tongue as tears streamed down her face. "Take him gently with both hands, Jesus," she wept. Unknowingly echoing the words of King David at the loss of his son thousands of years before, she continued in her tender voice, "Now he will no longer come to me but I will go to him."

Mahesh's heart broke at the sight of this woman's pure faith as he stepped outside and stood alone in the darkness. In our lives we have learned you can ask God, *Where? When? How? Who?* But the question *Why?* is different. That one is His to know and not ours to ask. Though Mahesh would not ask God why He did not resurrect the boy, he could not help feeling as though he had failed that poor mother. In that very moment, as his heart ached, a gentle wind surrounded him and out of it a Voice spoke.

Mahesh, as you have been faithful, you will see great things.

Some months later, back home, Mahesh received an invitation from a group of pastors in Zaire (now known as Congo). The letter, which was typed on a crumpled yellow piece of paper, was full of spelling mistakes. Some of the keys on the typewriter were clearly damaged. Yet when we read the plea for him to come and minister, we both sensed the voice of God. "We believe that if you will come," the letter said, "the destiny and future of our nation will be changed."

Our first thought was uncertainty that the authors of this letter could actually put together the outreach they were planning. "We expect hundreds of thousands in attendance and many, many lives will be changed," they wrote. We are never cavalier about missions, particularly when it risks the lives of believers, whether fathers, mothers or children. Yet we sensed the unction of the Holy Spirit in this invitation, so we did not immediately decline.

Mahesh had already made plans to return to Zambia where thousands had come to know Jesus and the miraculous power of God had healed bodies and lives. He still carried the agony of returning the lifeless body of the twin to his heartbroken mother. Although Zaire borders Zambia, we were pretty sure that the cost of adding a flight into that country would prevent us from accepting the invitation. You can imagine our surprise when the travel agent told us the new itinerary would only require 27 extra dollars! The Lord was answering loud and clear, and Mahesh accepted the invitation.

The Voice in the Storm

Shortly thereafter we received yet another surprise. I was expecting our fourth child. Within a few weeks, however, I was diagnosed with *placenta previa centralis*, a condition where the placenta, which nourishes the unborn child, covers the entire cervical opening. This places both the mother and baby at risk of death. This proved to be just the first band of rain as we headed into the storm.

After a number of tests the doctors essentially told us to abort our baby. They advised this out of concern for my life. They could find no sign of life in my womb, and assured us that if the baby was alive and lived through delivery, it would not survive past a few days. If it did live longer, it would be in a vegetative state. As if to confirm their fears, I began to hemorrhage. When we asked God what to do, however, we heard only silence. So we waited.

Over the next few weeks, Mahesh assumed the role of Mr. Mom, trying to run a household with three children under the age of seven. I was stuck in bed, only allowed to walk three steps to the bathroom and three steps back to bed. Dark clouds of depression and uncertainty began to gather around me. I tried my best to stay positive, confessing Scripture and reminding myself of God's faithfulness in the storm.

My body went wild with fluctuating hormone levels and bouts of premature labor. I was frustrated and bored nearly to tears: You can only read so many magazines! On the other hand, it was a struggle to stay in the place of *shalom*, resting in God's love for us in this crisis. In a drawn-out battle like this, it was essential that my mind and body remain strong for the duration of the pregnancy, rather than wear myself out through constant engagement in the spiritual war raging over the lives of my child and myself.

During those weeks, my eyes gravitated toward one of the gifts Mahesh had brought home from his latest trip to Africa: a small, handmade painting of an African man making his way through a dense green jungle. The image of the man was dark and small in the midst of the forest. When I looked at it, I remembered the stories of Mahesh's time there—how many who were sick and hungry had walked for days to come to hear the Gospel.

That little picture hung on the wall I passed while taking the three steps I was allowed to and from the bathroom. I thought of the women in difficulties like my own but without a modern home, a caring church family or good doctors to help them through. I determined not to waste my sorrows in pity for myself. The little man in the picture became the "bull's-eye" for my prayers. I may have been lying on my back in one of the greatest tests of my faith, but I could still pray!

And pray I did. As I continued to bleed, I prayed for miracles in the lives of needy Africans. With every racking cramp of false labor I asked the Lord to do something great for all those who had no other Helper. My bed of trouble became an aircraft carrier, launching rocket after rocket of Holy Ghost-loaded prayers into the heart of darkness. I was a storm warrior, and this storm was the place to "put up or shut up," as my cowboy ancestors would say.

I was 21 weeks pregnant and there were still no signs of life in my womb. We continued to wait for God to speak. He seemed to be hiding His face regarding our baby. When we had faced the life-and-death issues with our first son, Ben, I never imagined I would have to pass through that valley again. We were learning that God can use a previous victory in an even greater test of faith.

Mahesh also prayed with all his might day after day. One afternoon God spoke to him: *I will give you a secret weapon.* Mahesh waited, expecting a miracle just around the corner. Then he heard the most unusual thing: *You and Bonnie need to laugh your way through this.*

Mahesh's first reaction was to inform God that there was not a single part of the current circumstances that was remotely funny. But we also knew to obey. So Mahesh brought home audiotapes of one of our favorite comedians. For an hour or so each afternoon we would lie on our bed and listen to the antics of hilarious stories and laugh and laugh. We soon found we had more faith, more hope, more love and peace even though our circumstances continued to worsen. Then one day I heard that Voice.

You will have a son. His name is Aaron.

The Lord gave me Numbers 17:3–4, 7–8 to hold onto:

And you shall write Aaron's name on the rod of Levi. . . . Then you shall place them in the tabernacle of meeting before the Testimony, where I meet with you. . . . And Moses placed the rods before the LORD in the tabernacle of witness. Now it came to pass on the next day that Moses went into the tabernacle of witness, and behold, the rod of Aaron, of the house of Levi, had sprouted and put forth buds, had produced blossoms and yielded ripe almonds.

Could I believe it? Was God really going to give us a son when the doctors had yet to find a heartbeat? I hid this word deep in my heart.

The next week I got a phone call from a friend in Texas whom I had not spoken with in several years. "I was in my prayer closet," she said. "I have never gotten a word like this in my life, but I believe God spoke to me. He said you are going to have a son. You are supposed to name him Aaron." With this amazing confirmation, I could stand firmly on what God had promised and invite others to stand with me.

My body, however, had yet to believe. My water broke months early. The placenta had worked so hard while I was hemorrhaging that half of it broke off and fell out of my body. Over those weeks I died on two occasions. I experienced firsthand what people often describe upon returning from death—how the spirit leaves the body and observes the situation and persons left behind. As my spirit left my worn-out body, I looked down on my husband and children in our home and thought of how awful it would be for Mahesh to be left to handle our family alone. With the awareness of what our children would go through without their mother at their tender ages, I found I had the power to choose and willed myself to stay. I discovered how easy it is for a believer to step from this realm into the next. It was no more than a breath away!

Our doctor, a devout Indian Sikh, watched over me attentively and soon began to remark about our steady faith. "I have never met two people who are closer to Him," he told us one day. Though we were mostly preoccupied with our own trials, we soon realized others were watching. Our storm was becoming a testimony to the presence of the Lord.

Mahesh and I believed that he needed to fulfill every commitment to travel and preach what the Lord had put on our hearts. It happened, then, that as I entered my 25th week, Mahesh was not at home. I was admitted to the hospital and my doctor decided to do an emergency Caesarean. By now he had taken to sleeping on a cot in the hospital ward because of my precarious situation. He explained that he needed my husband's signature on the permission forms. When I told him that Mahesh was in the Antilles, he walked away shaking his head.

Surgery was planned around Mahesh's return home. The night before he was due back, I had an unusual dream. I was flying, tucked under the wing of a great bird. We traveled over wide expanses of pristine wilderness. Wildlife frolicked below us on snow-covered mountain slopes. I felt tremendous peace, joy and safety under the wing of the Great Bird and knew that it was He, the God of my salvation.

All of a sudden in the dream a sound emanated from the One who held me. It was not a song or words. It was more like beams of love, power, life and creation. It was the Voice of the Lord. As those waves of light and life reverberated, the mountains shook—and the side of the largest mountain slid away into a valley. I watched, in awe of His power. Then written across the sky of my dream were words from Psalm 29: "The voice of the LORD makes the deer give birth" (verse 9).

The next morning Mahesh returned, and I was rushed to surgery. The operating room was filled with more than two dozen medical personnel. Half of them were there to keep me alive, and half of them were there in case there was life in my womb. As they scurried about, the anesthesiologist prepared to put me to sleep. Just as he was about to administer the anesthesia, another Man entered the room. I perceived His form as He came to the head of the stretcher where I lay. I saw those same rays of light and love and power emanate from Him. They covered my head and traveled down my body. As they passed through my throat and into my chest and arms, I saw my hand lift up, and I heard myself announce to the doctor, "I can have this baby naturally."

My doctor took one look at me and stopped the movement in the room. "Okay," he said. I could not believe what I had just said, and I was even more shocked the doctors were listening to me! I thought frantically to myself, *Wait a minute. I do not want to have this baby naturally! Give me drugs!* Yet the Voice surrounded my womb and began to push. In moments I heard five little tiny mews like the sound of a newborn kitten.

I could not see what the obstetrician was holding in his hands, but I could see his face turn ashen and knew he was looking down at the child. Then I remembered the word of the Lord from before. "It's a boy, isn't it?" I declared more than asked. The doctor nodded his head.

"His name is Aaron. He will live and not die."

I did not wake again until the next day. Aaron weighed less than one pound. He had a staph infection, blood in his spinal fluid indicating a brain hemorrhage, and his lungs were not fully developed. His ears were still flaps of skin. His tiny face was smashed flat from the lack of amniotic fluid to cushion it. His dry skin was bruised everywhere. That was not even the worst of it. A portion of Aaron's intestines had died *in utero*. The calcification had perforated the part that was still alive, and he had developed gangrene in his body cavity. My wedding ring could fit onto his tiny leg. His fingertips were so small that his nails were invisible. This was the son of whom God had said He would "make his rod bud."

"You Will See Great Things"

In the midst of this crisis Mahesh was due to leave for Africa. It seemed that if he left he would never hold Aaron again in this life. When I learned he was planning to cancel the trip I asked him to reconsider. I recalled the simple plea the Zairian pastors had written on that crumpled sheet of paper and recounted the hours of prayer that I had lifted up for the African people. "Your presence here cannot make Aaron live or die. But you carry miracles. Your presence out there may mean life or death for someone else." With his heart breaking he left to proclaim the Good News to the poor in obedience to the call God had placed on our hearts.

As I battled day to day at home to see our son through, Mahesh preached the Gospel and prayed for the sick beneath the African sun. On a Wednesday just before noon as he stood before fifty thousand hungry people, the same wind that had surrounded Mahesh the previous year outside that hut in Zambia appeared again. It seemed to put his sur-roundings into slow motion and quiet the desperate masses in front of him. Then the Voice spoke. *There is a man here whose son died this morning. Call him up because today I am going to do a great thing.*

Stepping back to the microphone Mahesh gave the word of the Lord. "Where is that man?" he asked. Mulamba Manikai, tall and handsome, came running from the back of the crowd waving his arms to identify himself. As he leaped onto the platform he began explaining to interpreters that, indeed, his six-year-old son, Katshinyi, had died before dawn of cerebral malaria, the same disease that had taken the young woman's twin. The child was the same age that boy would have been. Katshinyi's lifeless body lay in the arms of a grieving uncle who was with the child's mother at Mama Yemo hospital in Kinshasa, Zaire.

Mahesh took the hands of Mulamba and prayed a simple prayer. "Lord, I pray that the same Spirit that raised Your

Son from the dead will go now and quicken the body of this man's son!" Several witnesses who were there in Mama Yemo that afternoon said that at just past noon the lifeless body of the boy suddenly sneezed twice and sat up in his uncle's arms! News of this miracle spread throughout the entire region, and there was tremendous rejoicing.

Yet that was not the end of the story.

The same glory that raised Katshinyi came home to us, and things finally began to turn around for Aaron. From death to life God healed Aaron completely. Today our son is an athletic, handsome, intelligent young man who loves and serves God.

From all of this, we have learned that God speaks to us out of His love for us. God's love for us moved Him to speak to us in our time of trouble. God's love for Aaron gave His voice words. God's love for Katshinyi made Him faithful to His promise to Mahesh. God's love for the mother and her sons in Zambia used their trial to spark thousands of other fires. Her son is alive with Jesus, and she will hold him in her arms, but her story, intertwined for eternity with ours, has been an ongoing catalyst for miracles. In her suffering, many mothers and fathers have found hope for their children.

In His love, He creates a calm place in the storm where we can find refuge and regain our strength.

The Still, Small Voice

You may be fighting for the life and destiny of someone you love. The still, small voice holds the key to victory. We must be able to hear Him in order to hold on to His living Word and obey even if He does not speak through "a burning bush" or bolt of lightning.

First Kings 19 tells the story of Elijah hearing God, not in a strong wind or earthquake or fire, but in a still, small voice. Translated from the Hebrew word *kol*, this alludes to the sound *mmm* made through closed lips. In the Hebrew tradition it expresses wonder and awe at the glory of God. Elijah was almost suicidal at this point in his life, and yet when he heard this voice his spirits were lifted immediately. His courage was revived, and he pressed on with his call. The still, small voice holds the answer in the storm.

Hearing God's direction and recognizing the still, small voice comes with practice. Mahesh can be in a crowd of five thousand people and still recognize my laugh. He *knows* my laugh. We develop the same ability to recognize the voice of the Lord through our ongoing relationship with Him. In a mystery, that intimacy is the dwelling place of miracles.

Again we see the importance of relationship. Spiritual vision is the optimism of heaven in the worst situation. It comes from the realm of faith that grows through our personal relationship with God. Without it we will succumb to the storm every time. This does not mean we ignore natural circumstances. God, in fact, often uses practical situations to bring us clarity. When Mahesh's new itinerary only cost 27 extra dollars, we took that as confirmation that God wanted him to go to Zaire. But when we have vision, optimism and certainty that God is involved, it will also open up our hearts to hear His voice when our circumstances do not seem to match up with the vision. He speaks into faith in the same way that He spoke the worlds into existence: by the word of His voice. "By faith we understand that the worlds were framed by the word of God, so that the things which are seen were not made of things which are visible" (Hebrews 11:3).

Here are four keys for the storm warrior who desires to find the calm and hear the still, small voice in the midst of it.

Stay Committed to Your Mission

The Lord graced Mahesh and me to hear His voice clearly as we stayed committed to His vision for souls in Africa in spite of our own personal storm. His vision is beyond our personal salvation. It is that the Gospel be spread to the nations, beginning with the people in our personal sphere. As we begin to ask the Lord to make us a testimony to those around us and focus on His purposes, we will receive greater clarity.

Song of Songs records the words of the Bridegroom to His lover: "Let me see your face, let me hear your voice." The heart that is "married" to the Lord "for better or for worse," even when it seems as though the situation is pointing to "worse," will hear His voice in the storm. God certainly did not move in my pregnancy with Aaron the way we might have assumed He would. Yet because we did not presume to know, we did not become bitter or crippled by disappointment.

What we did know we held on to: Our calling and commitment were to preach the Gospel. We knew that God had said yes to the trip to Africa before our personal situation grew in difficulty. When God seemed to remain silent about our immediate situation and my pregnancy spiraled into greater and greater peril, our commitment to the original word of direction He had given us became the rudder for our ship in that storm. While we never expected to experience the challenges we did with Aaron, that overarching commitment was the foundation for our faith and gave the Lord a clear channel to speak into our lives. We had already made the decision that our lives were a testimony that we "may know Him and the power of His resurrection, and the fellowship of His sufferings" (Philippians 3:10).

This is the mission for every believer: "And this gospel of the kingdom will be preached in all the world as a witness to all the nations, and then the end will come" (Matthew 24:14). It is the big picture, the eternal purpose of God that defines the temporal moments of our lives. That is how vision is clarified. Once we have a vision for the big picture, the storms of life become just dots along the map of our journey.

Use the Secret Weapon

The history of Christianity teaches us that when people are overcome with religion, they lose two things: the joy of living and the prophetic voice of God. Laughter is like good medicine. A principal expression of God's personality is joy. We can pick up the vibration from the realm of the eternal where He rules and be a "superconductor" of that strength in temporal life.

It was difficult for Mahesh and me not to get bogged down in the details as the storm of our circumstances raged unabated. It was a challenge not to slip into despair as I lay in my bed day in and day out. Both Mahesh and I were standing firm in our faith, obedient to the word the Lord had given us, but we needed to add a new weapon to our arsenal: joy!

During the time of Ezra and Nehemiah, the Israelites were struggling to restore Jerusalem after their exile. Remembering her former glory and seeing how far they had fallen, the people wept and cried as Ezra read from the Law. Their mission looked impossible in their existing situation. Not only was their city in physical ruin, but they saw that they were also in spiritual disrepair. But Nehemiah encouraged them: "Go your way, eat the fat, drink the sweet . . . for this day is holy to our Lord. Do not sorrow, for the joy of the LORD is your strength" (Nehemiah 8:10).

Their eyes were focused on the wrong picture: themselves, their failures and their challenges. They missed the big picture: God was miraculously restoring them to the mission to which He had first called them. That joy would be the strength for the journey that lay ahead.

The joy of the Lord is our strength, and there is no greater need for strength than times of testing. There is a release of spiritual power in the laughter that comes from faith. "He who sits in the heavens shall laugh" (Psalm 2:4) and triumph over His enemies. The heavenly perspective is a joyous one. It is based on the finished work of Jesus Christ, who is seated at the right hand of the Father above every power and principality (see Ephesians 1:20-21). Because He has triumphed, we can laugh at the devices of the enemy. In our case, we needed something completely "unspiritual," the comic antics of a comedian we enjoyed, to prime the pump of our emotions. Laughter loosed the river of joy and brought us into a revival of hope.

Joy is the storm warrior's secret weapon! Laughter breaks Satan's hold on our emotions and releases us from the clutches of fear. It shifts the atmosphere of our circumstances from despair and heaviness and opens the way for hope to permeate our surroundings.

While our circumstances only grew direr, our faith and hope increased as we made this secret weapon a part of our daily routine. The atmosphere around us began to change, and it was at that time that I heard the Lord speak, *You will have a son.*

Believe the Report of the Lord

A storm warrior believes the report of the Lord even when everyone else's voice seems to be louder. When every doctor was saying our son would never live, we held on to the report of the Lord: He will live and not die! We did not allow the circumstances to impede Mahesh from bringing the Gospel to those in even more desperate circumstances than ours. As Mahesh was faithful to the mission God had given us, the anointing that raised young Katshinyi from the dead ultimately raised our own son as well!

The reality of a true word from the glory is that it contains the power of resurrection for any and every situation. Once it is loosed, like light and sound waves flashing forth into space, it continues to move with the divine purpose of God.

Hebrews 10:35–38 tells us, "Therefore do not cast away your confidence, which has great reward. For you have need of endurance, so that after you have done the will of God, you may receive the promise." Even when deep darkness covers the earth, God promises that His glory will rise upon us. In His wings He brings healing, deliverance and restoration. In this glory is power and provision. We remember the words of Habakkuk: "The just shall live by faith."

God's voice calls forth things that are not into being and breathes resurrection life into promises that seem long dead.

Learn to Listen

Hearing and responding to God is an ongoing process. No one gets it right all the time. Still, we have His promise that

"My sheep hear My voice" (John 10:27). It is God's intention that all believers hear Him.

One of the tools that the Lord will use to fine-tune our hearing is confirmation from other sheep within His fold. The guidance of mature mothers and fathers of faith is important as we learn to hear and recognize the voice of the Lord. When my friend called from Texas with her word concerning our son, it was the confirmation that encouraged and equipped me for the battle that still lay ahead. There is no "army of one"; Scripture says we wage a good warfare by many counsels. That counsel is best heard through the mature in the faith who have been given a position of leadership in our lives.

When Samuel first heard the voice of the Lord, he did not recognize that it was God.

> Therefore Eli said to Samuel, "Go, lie down; and it shall be, if He calls you, that you must say, '*Speak, LORD, for Your servant hears.*'" So Samuel went and lay down in his place. Now the LORD came and stood and called as at other times, "Samuel! Samuel!" And Samuel answered, "Speak, for Your servant hears."
>
> 1 Samuel 3:9–10, emphasis added

Eli was Samuel's spiritual mentor. His confirmation that this was the voice of God helped Samuel hear and respond.

A second tool for fine-tuning our hearing is praying in the Spirit. God speaks to us Spirit to spirit. Often the voice of the Lord will come first through the spirit and then come to the mind. God is always speaking. Psalm 19 tells us that creation declares His glory and knowledge. We just do not always recognize Him. Praying in the Spirit is one of the best ways to increase the accuracy and sensitivity of our spiritual ears. It awakens our heart to His voice.

We encourage believers to begin setting aside time every day just to pray in the Spirit. This is not primarily a time of intense prayer or warfare, though that may occur. Communion with God through praying in the Spirit is like blood pumping through your heart, gathering nutrients to infuse the rest of your body. Your prayer language is God's delivery system. It awakens your ear to hear. As you develop a life of communing with Him—Spirit to spirit—His voice will flow like a river.

The third tool for learning to hear, test and recognize the voice of the Lord is His Word, the Scriptures.

The testimony of Jesus is the spirit of prophecy. Jesus is the Word made flesh. Every true word of prophecy and instruction will line up with His Word and His nature. The more familiar we are with His written Word, the more we can recognize when He speaks. Read the Word, enjoy the Word, chew the Word, enter into it and let it enter you. Then whenever you hear words of counsel or direction, whether directly to your spirit or through the voices of others, the quality and tone will alert you to the source.

Knowing the Word, praying continually in the Spirit and being submitted to the authority and mentoring of our spiritual family teaches us the basic vocabulary of how God speaks. The more we practice, the more clearly we hear and the more readily we recognize and obey. Hearing and responding to His voice makes us available to the Holy Spirit as ambassadors for His Kingdom on earth.

His Eye Is on the Sparrow

There was an element in my dream on the night before Aaron was born that puzzled me for many years afterward. The Great Bird under whose wings I flew was not the mighty eagle or any bird of strength and power one would expect. Granted, He was huge, but completely gentle in nature. That Great Bird was, in fact, a sparrow!

Years later, but as though not a day had passed, God spoke to my heart about the image of that bird. *My eye was on the tiny helpless being I had purposed to knit together in your womb.* I heard the words from a great old hymn: "His eye is on the sparrow, and I know He watches me." And then I thought of what Jesus said in the Bible: "Are not two sparrows sold for a copper coin? And not one of them falls to the ground apart from your Father's will. But the very hairs of your head are all numbered. Do not fear therefore; you are of more value than many sparrows" (Matthew 10:29–31).

John testified of Jesus, "Behold the Lamb of God who takes away the sin of the world." Then John saw the Spirit of God descend from heaven and remain upon Jesus (see John 1:29–30). The presence and power of the Spirit will come down to light upon those who have the nature of the Lamb. And as we stay humble before God the anointing of His Spirit will grow ever stronger. You can be sure that if God keeps an eye out for every tiny bird that falters, He certainly has an eye of love and care trained on you! You will have His calm in the storm.

6

Angels in the Storm

So bless God, you angels, ready and able to fly at his bidding.

Psalm 103:20, Message

I, Mahesh, will never forget the day of the great tornado of 1970, my first encounter with one of the supernatural beings known as angels. Torrential sheets of rain soaked through my light coat as I emerged that evening from the Texas Tech Library. It was May and I was attending graduate school. Exhausted from nearly twelve hours of study, I trudged the six blocks to my apartment amidst claps of thunder and gusts of wind.

Miserable but too tired even to change out of my wet clothing, I collapsed onto my well-worn couch. It was nine o'clock, and I hoped to relax for a while before heading to bed. I flipped on the television and began to watch an ABC special called "The Eye of the Storm." To this day, I can still see the title framed in my small television set.

Suddenly, about half an hour into the program, all the lights went out. Still in a daze from my intense studies, I did not even get up to find a flashlight or a candle. I just sat there in the dark, staring in the direction of the now-blank television screen. I had just resigned myself to dozing on the couch until the power came back on, when out of the darkness I heard a loud voice say, "Get up."

I was jolted to attention. Had I fallen asleep and dreamed? Was someone else there with me? Finally I concluded that I must be hallucinating from my exhaustion and allowed my body to relax back into the couch.

Again I heard the voice, "Get up!"

This is weird, I thought. The power was out, the television was off and I was definitely hearing voices.

A third time, more insistent than before, the voice said, *"Get up!"*

I was quite intellectual during that phase of my life, and to my rational mind it was one thing to *hear* voices. That generally meant you were going a little crazy. But if you went so far as to answer them, you were ready for the nice men in white to come and take you away! Yet for all my rational musings, I answered the voice out loud, "I'm tired!"

All at once I felt powerful hands grab me and lift me off the couch. I still could not see anyone; nonetheless, I was being held in the air with my feet literally dangling below me. I was incredulous. I struggled to free myself from its grip.

Within seconds I found myself plunked down behind my couch. Still resisting, as the presence pushed me down to the floor, I reached up and grabbed the back of the couch. Just then I heard a sound like a hundred trains coming toward my apartment, followed by an explosion of glass all around me. The next thing I knew, my hand was throbbing where the plate glass window from my front door sliced it on its flight across the room.

The famous 1970 Lubbock tornado, the most powerful tornado ever to strike the Southwest, had just passed through my neighborhood. Twenty-six people died that night, and more than fifteen hundred were injured. The F5 tornado cut a one-and-a-half-mile path of destruction through the city, flattening buildings and reducing whole areas to piles of rubble.

When I surveyed the damage to my apartment by morning's light, I was horrified. A huge shard of glass, the same one that had injured my hand, was embedded in the wall right where my head would have been. The presence that I had struggled with had literally saved my life.

Even though I was steeped in intellectualism and had no intention of going into ministry, God had a call on my life. He knew that He was going to use me to bring more than a million souls to Jesus Christ. The small scar, still visible on my knuckle today, is a testament that the Lord sent an angel to protect me. That encounter with one of God's mighty messengers made me aware of the very real help Christians have on hand during the storms we encounter.

Angels of God are involved in the everyday affairs of men on earth. The Bible says they are "ministering spirits sent forth to minister for those who will inherit salvation" (Hebrews 1:14). Abraham, Daniel, Mary, the shepherds of Bethlehem, Jesus during His ministry on earth and many others in Scripture encountered angelic messengers sent to fulfill the word of God in answer to prayers.

God desires to open our eyes to the awesome power of His heavenly messengers and awaken His Church to the vital role they play in God's mission of salvation. Our God commissions heavenly messengers to guard and protect us, assist and deliver us, comfort and strengthen us. As we face natural and spiritual battles, there is an unseen army in company with all who do God's will. They are His army of heavenly envoys created and commissioned to aid those who call on the name of the Lord.

Angels in the Bible

There are more than three hundred accounts of angels recorded in the Bible. We see that they have a voice, a personality, a will and a spiritual body all to do God's good pleasure. At times they appear as humans, even someone we may know, as in the case of Peter on the night the church was watching and praying. The ministry of angels surrounds the exaltation of Jesus past, present and future in heaven and on earth.

In the ancient journal of Job, angels were on hand in the great struggle between the forces of good and evil. When Lot was surrounded by wickedness in Sodom, angels came knocking. Elijah despaired for his life until the Lord of Hosts sent angels to strengthen him. When the false prophet Balaam was summoned to curse Israel, an angel interrupted his journey by appearing to his donkey long before Balaam figured out what was going on.

The strategic name for God throughout the Bible is the *Lord of Hosts*, literally the *Lord of Armies*. I like this description in *The Message*:

GOD! Let the cosmos praise your wonderful ways, the choir of holy angels sing anthems to your faithful ways! Search

high and low, scan skies and land, you'll find nothing and no
one quite like GOD. The holy angels are in awe before him;
he looms immense and august over everyone around him.
GOD-of-the-Angel-Armies, who is like you, powerful and
faithful from every angle? You put the arrogant ocean in its
place and calm its waves when they turn unruly.

Psalm 89:5–9

Sometimes humans take a part among these military
ranks under God-of-the-Angel-Armies. When Deborah
and Barak went into battle against Sisera, angels—as well
as stars and rivers!—entered the action. When Herod murdered the apostle James and then planned to do the same to
Peter, the Church prayed and God sent an angel to deliver
His servant from chains. In the Revelation of Jesus Christ,
the apostle John saw the Lord of Armies, Jesus, as the Lamb
"who in righteousness judges and makes war." With Him
were hosts of angels.

These are just some examples from the biblical record of
angels on assignment, helping God's people during times of
trouble. Some of the most famous accounts of these visita-
tions were to men and women who do not necessarily fit
our description of mighty servants of God. After deceiv-
ing his father and taking his brother's blessing, Jacob fled
for his life. On Jacob's first night on the run God opened
the heavens and Jacob saw angels passing between heaven
and earth on their mission. They did not come because of
Jacob's righteousness, but because they were faithful messengers of God and defenders of His covenant with Abraham's descendants.

Here are some important scriptural truths about angels:

Angels have great knowledge but are not omniscient and are not to be worshiped (see 1 Peter 3:22; Revelation 22:8–9).

Angels were created through the Son of God (see Colossians 1:16).

Angels are great in might and power (see Acts 5:19; 2 Thessalonians 1:7).

Angels excel in strength (see Psalm 103:20).

Angels are active in the lives of individuals, families, churches, cities and nations (see Daniel 10:10–14; Revelation 2:1).

Angels watch over our children (see Matthew 18:10).

Angels do not marry or die (see Matthew 22:30).

Angels are glorious beings (see Daniel 6; Matthew 28:2–3).

Angels can listen to our conversations (see Daniel 10:12).

Angels have ranks and orders, all of which are subject to Jesus Christ (see Hebrews 1:6).

Angels exist in countless numbers (see Hebrews 12:22).

Angels are ministering spirits to assist the heirs of salvation (see 1 Kings 19:5–8; 2 Kings 6:15–17; Psalm 91:11–12; Acts 5:19; 12:8–11; 27:23–24).

Angels offer comfort to God's people in times of trouble (see Luke 1:11).

Angels can carry out the judgments of God (see Genesis 19:13; Matthew 13:47–50; Revelation 15:1) or rescue people from danger (see Genesis 19; Acts 12).

Angels surround and protect those who fear the Lord (see Psalm 34:7).

Angels receive the spirits of righteous people at their deaths (see Luke 16:22).

Angels rejoice when we repent (see Luke 15:10).

Angels will accompany the Lord when He returns to the earth (see Matthew 25:31–32).

Angels will separate the children of the Kingdom from the children of the wicked one (see Matthew 13:41).

Angels show up in direct answer to prayer (see Acts 10).

Angels are awesome, mighty and powerful beings (see Psalm 103:20).

Angels guard the city gates of God (see Revelation 21:12).

Angels deliver God's healing grace (see John 5).

Angels have been seen by men (see Genesis 32:1–2; Daniel 10:6; Luke 2:9,13; John 20:12).

Angels dwell in heaven (see Luke 2:13, 15).

Angels bring refreshment to the saints who are engaged in spiritual battle (see Daniel 10:17–19).

The Bible shows that angels break into our natural circumstances, bringing supernatural intervention from on high so that we might fulfill God's destiny in difficult times as well as happy ones. War, worship, proclamation of salvation, deliverance from disaster and victory over enemies are all characteristics of the circumstances in which we find angels at work.

We see, further, that their proclamations will always be consistent with the prophetic purpose of God as revealed in His Word. Holy angels will never reveal anyone but Jesus Christ as the Savior and Lord of all (see Galatians 1:8). They will never receive worship from humans or other angels.

They are servant messengers and ministers assigned by God to help care for His saints.

Angels Carry the Glory

Miracles of healing and deliverance are among the primary manifestations of God's Kingdom on earth. Angels are sent to assist in that great work by carrying the glory from the throne into our circumstances. The angel that stirred the pool of Bethesda, for instance, was a carrier of God's healing presence. That messenger was saturated in the glory from communion with God. He then transmitted the Lord's glory and virtue to those waters. When he entered the pool, the water was stirred by those waves or vibrations of glory and danced with God's presence and power. As the infirm got into the pool they were restored to health and wholeness.

Often in our healing services we become aware of the presence of angels. These mighty, holy, spiritual beings carry the vibration of power straight from the throne. I, Mahesh, can sometimes hear it; it sounds like a mighty hum. I know when I hear that sound the atmosphere around us has changed, and we have crossed into the realm where nothing is impossible. In that realm supernatural knowledge also becomes clear. God will give names of persons needing His touch and words of knowledge about infirmities or particular challenges in the lives of those present. As we declare those words from the glory, people are healed and delivered.

I was ministering in Budapest, Hungary, shortly after the Soviet Union dissolved and Communism fell. I was in terrible pain physically because I had torn the meniscus in my knee; I was due to have surgery as soon as I returned to the United States. The first miracle was that the pain in my knee became secondary as the meeting proceeded. In spite of the difficulty I had walking, supernatural strength from the presence of ministering angels helped me as I wound my way around the giant coliseum. I laid hands on nearly fourteen thousand people that day!

At the beginning of the ministry time God whispered to me His desire to deliver these precious believers from the dark shadows that the constant oppression of Communism had left on their society. I got a word of knowledge that many people there were suffering from depression and had attempted suicide. When I called them forward, more than one thousand people came. I closed my eyes to pray and took authority over the suicide and depression. As soon as I said "in Jesus' name" I opened my eyes to find that the whole mass of people had been knocked to the floor by the power of God. They began to receive deliverance and healing. When I spoke the word, angels responded to His command and brought deliverance from the throne to all who had come forward.

How to Invite Angelic Intervention

We invite intervention and ministry of angels when we are aligned with the purposes and will of our heavenly Father. Often when the anointing of the Holy Spirit is on a particular word of healing or other miracle there will be a release of angelic activity that brings sudden breakthrough. Time and again we have witnessed this when families and individuals stand their ground believing God for a miracle.

The elderly priest Zacharias was offering incense on the altar of prayer when he was startled by an angel's sudden appearance. "Do not be afraid, Zacharias, for your prayer is heard; and your wife Elizabeth will bear you a son, and you shall call his name John" (Luke 1:13). Zacharias was so old that all hope of answer to his prayers to have a child of his own had passed many years before. But God had not forgotten. Zacharias was to father one who would prepare the way for God's Son. He sent His angel Gabriel to announce this to the priest. The announcement of the word loosed the miracle of its fulfillment. Within weeks Elizabeth discovered she was pregnant.

Angelic activity is entwined with the prayers of God's people. Or, to put it another way, praying people will have angelic activity in the events of their lives. Zacharias and Elizabeth waited until it seemed impossible for their prayer to be answered, but the word was delivered and the miracle followed immediately.

Sometimes when we are in a battle, the anointed word of the Lord will loose angels and secure the victory as we speak. Other times the Word becomes the target for our consistent prayers. The enemy will try to discourage and oppose us in the very place that the Lord has given us direction. But persistent, consistent, faith-filled prayer will prevail and loose the miracle for our deliverance. His word will not return void. His angels are instruments of power to fulfill it.

Our obedience to move forward or to hold our ground according to the word of the Lord will loose angels to come to our aid. Psalm 91:11–12: "For He shall give His angels charge over you, to keep you in all your ways. In their hands they shall bear you up, lest you dash your foot against a stone." In the midst of a crisis, when it looks as if the enemy of our soul has overwhelmed us, holding on to God's truth will release these powerful angels into our situations.

Several years ago I, Mahesh, preached at a crusade in the city of Abidjan in the Ivory Coast. During the evening meeting God granted a wonderful miracle. A young boy who had been crippled started to walk. His uncle was a policeman and happened to be there on duty during the event. He came up to me afterward, moved to tears. "This is my nephew. He has always been a cripple, and here he is. He has been healed!"

One of the government cabinet ministers was also a witness to this miracle. He was touched by the uncle's testimony. It gave him fresh hope for his own daughter, who was bound and crippled in a very different way. The next day, he came with his entire family and asked if they could have a brief time with me after the morning meeting. I sat down with them as soon as the meeting was over.

The grandmother became the spokesperson because the rest of the family began weeping uncontrollably. She showed me a picture of a smiling young woman. "This is my granddaughter Angela. My son's daughter. We sent her to Paris, France, to study at the university." The grandmother continued to explain how once there, Angela somehow got into drugs and then, running out of money to buy them, turned to prostitution. Soon she was trapped in that lifestyle, and they had not heard from her for a few years.

The close-knit family was completely devastated. They felt certain their sweet Angela would die alone in the streets of Paris and they would never see her again. In the midst of their sobs I looked at the picture of Angela. As I saw her lovely face something rose up in me. I snatched the picture of Angela from her grandmother. "Grandma," I said, "this is not a time to cry. This is a time to fight!"

99

And fight we did. They agreed in prayer as I bound the powers of seduction and addiction holding Angela captive thousands of miles away from where we stood. In the name of Jesus I commanded demons to loose her and I prayed that she would see the light of God. Then I charged, "Angels of God, go and rescue Angela!"

The family's weeping subsided, and they left our time together encouraged.

That evening they came back to the meeting beaming with joy. A few hours after I had prayed, Angela had called them! She was crying and said, "Papa, I want to come home. Send me a ticket. I have had enough of this life and I want to come home." Her father sent her a plane ticket and she came home that very week to Abidjan.

Prayer is the first assignment of the Church. It routes armies and defeats principalities, making way for the effective advance of the Gospel of Jesus Christ to the ends of the earth. We have been given the ability in prayer to loose angels and to extend the Kingdom of God in these tumultuous times. His angels work together with our prayers to set the captives free.

Guardians of Nations

The story of Daniel tells us a great deal about the global interaction of angels. Daniel lived out his days in captivity in Babylon, but his prayers transcended his physical circumstances. He refused to allow his spirit and mind to be bound by the confines of his physical body in exile or the repression of a pagan king.

Daniel teaches us, first of all, that prayer and fasting can loose angelic activity to the point of moving heaven and earth. As Daniel humbled himself in fasting and prayer, the angel Gabriel came in response. Daniel became a point of contact for the messenger from heaven to reveal God's redemptive plan for the whole nation in that hour.

> And he said to me, "O Daniel, man greatly beloved, understand the words that I speak to you, and stand upright, for I have now been sent to you." While he was speaking this word to me, I stood trembling. Then he said to me, "Do not fear, Daniel, for from the first day that you set your heart to understand, and to humble yourself before your God, your words were heard; and I have come because of your words. . . . Now I have come to make you understand what will happen to your people in the latter days, for the vision refers to many days yet to come."
>
> Daniel 10:11–12, 14

Daniel's account is one of the most insightful to teach us about the war being waged in the spiritual realm. As the story unfolds we learn that principalities and forces of spiritual wickedness in high places are able to resist the saints of God and the will of God on earth. When Jesus died on the cross, the legal power of those evil princes was broken. The devil has not yet conceded his defeat, however, and so he continues to enslave and hold captive all he can seduce, deceive or imprison.

This means that human administrations are subject to this ongoing spiritual and natural battle for control of the earth. Demonic princes have settled in over many nations' affairs and rule through ungodly persons holding governmental authority. In Daniel's case, Alexander conquered the kingdom of Babylon and domain was passed from one demonic prince to another. Daniel entered the battle as an ambassador of God. By prayer and fasting he pierced the darkness overhead and opened the way for the archangel Gabriel to come with a message. Those prayers also brought Michael to fight for God's purposes, as we will see in a moment. God's holy angels passed between heaven and earth to uphold His plan in response to Daniel's prayers.

Just as there are rulers of wickedness over nations, so do nations have angels assigned to them to fight for God's righteous cause. Many nations are the focus of a wrestling match between light and darkness. God is awakening Christians as watchmen for their nations, deploying us in prayer, fasting and proclaiming the Gospel. God has predetermined the boundaries of the nations and those who dwell in them that we might seek and find the Lord (see Acts 17:26). As active citizens we must pray and fast for our nations as part of our personal spiritual call to faithfulness.

What happens in the politics of your nation affects, and is affected by, you. Part of your spiritual calling is authority as an ambassador of heaven within the boundaries of your national citizenship. Pray that good men and women will rule in your nation so that holy angels will have access to and influence in your land. Pray that your national leaders will be servants of the Lord and friends of Israel. In fact, a sure way to bring blessing to a nation is for the saints to intervene in prayer not only for the peace of Jerusalem but also for their nations to be friends of Israel.

Many nations are in danger because of their blindness regarding blessing Israel. One of God's eternal promises is His covenant with the descendants of Abraham through his son Isaac. That promise holds for the Jewish people in every generation—including this one. One of the essential revelations for every Gentile believer is the fact that we have been grafted in to an ancient Jewish root.

The international crisis of Daniel's day had a direct bearing on the nation of Israel. The archangel Michael is called Israel's "prince," meaning one with governmental authority who "stands up" for God's people—in this case the Jews—in a time of trouble. God defends Israel from her enemies and blesses those who bless her. He has assigned the archangel Michael as the special protector of the nation of Israel. Considering the fact that one angel in Scripture could slay ten thousand with one blow, we should fear to touch the apple of God's eye through any national or international means.

We get a clearer focus of this picture in the story of Joshua entering the plain outside of Jericho. He encountered there an "Angel" standing with His sword drawn for battle. Joshua asked, "Are you for us or against us?" The Angel explained that He was not following Joshua but that He was the Captain. "As Commander of the army of the LORD I have now come" (Joshua 5:14). The Angel in this case was not one of the innumerable created hosts who are servant ministers but the pre-incarnate Christ. Jesus appeared several times to saints in the Old Testament as *the* Angel or Chief Messenger of the Lord. As Joshua stepped out in obedience, Jesus Himself came at the head of the ranks of angels to help the descendants of Abraham take ownership of Israel, according to God's promise.

We know many firsthand reports of angelic intervention in the battle for Israel still today. Our friend Tsvi, who served in the Israel Defense Force, told us of an amazing victory made possible with the help of angels on assignment. He was one of only a hundred Israeli soldiers left to defend an outpost in the Sinai, guarding the southern entrance to

Israel. They watched as Egyptian tanks filled the plain below their post. The Israeli soldiers went on high alert, ready to defend their position 24/7 for the first few days of the Egyptian mobilization. The Israeli soldiers were outnumbered and had only a limited amount of ammunition left. With tension mounting, they waited.

Days passed and the Egyptians did not make a move to strike. Puzzled, the Israelis continued to watch, but began to allow soldiers to sleep in shifts. Finally, to their amazement and relief, the thousands of invaders suddenly turned and retreated. That tiny outpost was the only natural barrier between Israel and the invading army, but they turned back home without a fight. Our friend told us that it was just like in the Bible. God sent His invisible forces to stand before them and confuse the mind of the enemy. God-of-the-Angel-Armies is now turning His heart toward "home" to keep His promise to gather Israel into His bosom as He told Abraham He would do thousands of years ago.

The battle is fierce—particularly in places where an antichrist spirit, pagan or secular humanist religions, violence or poverty have pervaded a culture for centuries. But angels on assignment work with the prayers of the saints to overturn wickedness and restore righteousness to human governments. The result is a peaceful land where the Gospel may go forth freely. The glory of every nation that has been washed in the blood of the Lamb will be on display in the eternal city of God. The leaders, customs and cultures blessed by the Father shall give honor and glory to Him as they stream into the New Jerusalem (see Revelation 21:24–26).

As it was in the days of Daniel, angels are all around us. Many are waiting for our prayers to loose them according to the will of God. We can invite their ministry now as we head into end time storms. God-of-the-Angel-Armies is our refuge and ark of safety. His hosts are here to do His will.

Preparation for His Coming

Scripture reveals that angelic activity increased with the advent of Jesus on earth. Angels are familiar players in the stories of His birth, death and resurrection. Likewise, a third of the chapters in the book of Acts mention angels. In John's Revelation, Jesus addresses personal letters of instruction and encouragement to the messenger angels who serve local church congregations facing various trials and challenges.

We also see in Revelation a prophetic picture of Him opening the seals of a scroll that He receives from the right hand of God the Father. Those seals are not unlike labor contractions: the inevitable prelude to birth. They commence the arrival of particular events—political, environmental and economic—upon the earth. This is the work of God-of-the-Angel-Armies whom we serve. His hosts are coming forth in preparation for the next revelation of Christ from heaven.

Complete authority over the kingdoms of the earth has been given to Christ. The eyes of God are on His saints on earth, and His ear is open to their prayers as He reigns. It seems He has a predetermined plan of action to bring justice and peace, and all the while His attention is concentrated on His people as they proceed through the last days before His coming. As the earth rocks along in her labor, Jesus is lining up rank after rank of His angelic forces in preparation for His return. At that time the graves of earth will all open because of the cosmic power of the Risen Christ over every dead thing.

The first and last words that God-of-the-Angel-Armies directs His faithful old friend John to write down are "Grace and peace" and "I am coming soon"! So then let everyone who hears His voice today prepare himself. It is time to awaken from slumber. It is time to put off the old things and be filled with the Spirit.

"So bless God, you angels, ready and able to fly at his bidding" (Psalm 103:20, Message). Angels are on assignment with us. Let us invite their ministry as we head into end time storms.

7

Transformation
in the Storm

But we all, with unveiled face, beholding as in a mirror the glory of the Lord, are being transformed into the same image from glory to glory, just as by the Spirit of the Lord.

2 Corinthians 3:18

There are demonic storms and there are storms that are the result of the glory of God colliding with opposition to His Kingdom. No matter the source, storms stir things up. They rearrange our thoughts, change our priorities and alter our lives. The storms of life disrupt the status quo. But on the other hand, they cause us to depend on the Holy Spirit in new and greater ways. Jesus told His disciples that His return would be preceded by times of great peril and turmoil. Our heavenly Father intends that every storm, be it of glory or opposition, transform us.

The Prayer of Transformation

Together with our church family, Mahesh and I had gone to see the movie *The Passion of the Christ*. The scenes of Jesus' trial, agony in the Garden, arrest and crucifixion were powerfully imprinted on my mind. As we came home I was overcome with a desire to go to the mountain of prayer. A fresh sense of the depth of God's love lay upon my heart as I recalled Jesus' sacrifice. I went out for a prayer walk.

The night was clear with stars overhead as I turned down the road leading out of our neighborhood. Tears streamed down my face as I was caught up in the reality of the splendor and spectacle of Calvary. My heart was captivated afresh by the intervention of great love that promises ultimate triumph over sin and the grave!

Replaying the scenes of Jesus' prayer in Gethsemane, I paused on the portrayal of His rising after His prayerful agony. Having folded Himself body, mind and spirit into the Father's hand, it showed Jesus standing and taking a single step. As His sandaled foot met the earth it came down upon the head of a serpent that had been lingering nearby during His travail. The skull of the snake cracked and was crushed under Christ's heel—all because of a simple step on the path of obedience to the Father.

The reality of that power of Christ welled up within me as I walked along. I began to worship Him and pray in my prayer language. The moment I uttered the first sound I could see with spiritual eyes the presence of a mighty gathering army of the Lord's hosts in the air overhead. An army was mustering to the cry of my heart. It was like the story of Elisha and his servant as an opposing army surrounded the city where they stayed. There were two armies, but the servant with natural eyes only saw one. He panicked and thought all was lost. But the man of God replied, "No worries!" He prayed that the servant would see with true eyes, and ranks of spiritual warriors of light that had gathered on their behalf came into view: "And behold, the mountain was full of horses and chariots of fire all around Elisha" (2 Kings 6:17).

As I walked along praying in the Spirit I, too, beheld them—angels and saints that have gone on to glory all mounted on horses coming from the heavens! They were ready to overturn the forces of darkness on the word of my prayers.

In that moment I realized that I was an ambassador for the Church in this generation. God was listening for the voice of His Bride—and was ready to answer when she called! I was a vessel of incense, pouring out many prayers formed in the watches of the night by prayer groups around the world. As I was carried along with a heavenly gathering behind me, I thought of the soldiers serving on foreign fields in the global war on terror. Suddenly I saw a flash of light. I discerned that it shot in an arc from where I was walking over to a military base on the other side of the world where someone dear to us was serving. I felt that the prayers going up for him were being answered and that a breakthrough and time of refreshing was coming. It seemed that many prayers of many watches were suddenly being poured out for answers.

At an intersection in the road I heard the sound of several huge tractor trailer trucks roaring up the highway. I turned to discover that it was not trucks at all. I saw the effects of a fierce wind barreling down the valley toward me. In a moment it was upon me. Leaves and debris intermingled with stinging bursts of rain came from all directions. I could scarcely stand in its force. The gusting wind and rain and flying debris seemed the only rebuttal the prince of the power of the air could make to contradict prayers being loosed in the name of Jesus and the power of His blood! I began to laugh in triumph in the face of the wind and rain.

I pressed on in the wild storm and realized only later how dangerous that could have been. I was too busy singing Scripture to notice. "The Spirit of the Lord God is upon me because He has anointed me to preach good news!" I sang. "This is the year of the favor of the Lord! This is the day of the vengeance of our God!" When it occurred to me there was no other person or vehicle out on the street, I wondered if I should turn back. But then I saw something else. Before me in a vision on either side of the sidewalk were two great looming trees. As I moved between them words from the book of Jude came to mind. I saw those trees as symbols of two evils sinking their ideology into the hearts and minds of a new generation of young Americans.

The unction to uproot those trees and deliver the young generation was so strong I called them by name: "You twice-dead trees of perversion and rebellion, I pull you up out of the heart and soul of America by the root." As words from Scripture came to mind I reached out and "uprooted" each of the trees in succession. I bound the powers of deception and seduction rampant in the secular culture invading our college campuses. At that instant there was a huge cracking and crashing sound, and every streetlight for blocks in every direction suddenly went black!

By now I was drenched. With rain whipping my face, I made a "visor" over my eyes with my hands and distinguished a single pair of headlights creeping along the road.

The car stopped beside me. "Mom?" It was our daughter Serah who had come out in the storm to look for me. Grateful to be out of the elements, I got in the car, and as we turned for home I began to tell her about my unusual experience. Just as I was recounting the crashing sound of the trees in the vision, our headlights illuminated an astounding sight. There, lying across the highway, were two gigantic upturned trees. The crash I heard as I "uprooted" the spiritual trees trying to take root in a new generation was the sound of those two enormous trees being ripped out of the ground in the wind!

When we finally reached home I recounted the story once more to the rest of my family. The telephone rang. It was the young soldier I had prayed for when I saw the arc of light go to his military base on the other side of the world.

"How are you able to call? What's happening?" I asked.

"A little while ago," he said, "the power on the entire military base shut down. We got permission to come outside and use our cell phones while they try to restore power to our station."

I knew that God was giving us a sign to reinforce our belief that prayers in Jesus' name are mighty. They are heard on high. They are attended by angels. They shake things in heaven and change things on earth.

The next morning we went out to see the aftermath of the storm. Blocking the highway lay the two trees, each measuring more than seventy feet in height! In the months that followed we began to see powerful breakthrough and transformation in the lives of young people we had been interceding for. These children of believing parents began to turn away from darkness and back to the Lord and His plan for their lives. The roots of bondage were being broken.

Blessed and Broken

Storms in our lives, including the troubling events of our day, are meant for our transformation into the image of Jesus' glory. Pain is not meant to snuff out our lamps; pain is the oil that makes the flame burn brighter. Saint Francis of Assisi is quoted as saying, "And in dying, we behold His glory." It is the eternal law of redemption.

Sometimes the breaking is voluntary, as Jesus showed us by laying down His life in obedience to the Father. Matthew 26:26 says this: "As they were eating, Jesus took bread, blessed and broke it, and gave it to the disciples." Jesus' body was about to be broken on the cross. Because of His willing sacrifice, we can partake of His broken body, share in His suffering and multiply that life to others.

Later that night in the Garden, when Judas came to betray Jesus with an army behind him, Jesus called him "friend." In John 6:70, Jesus identified Judas as a devil. In John 12:6 He called him a thief. But on the night of His betrayal, He saw Judas as a vehicle of God's mission. The men who came to arrest Jesus were facilitating the plan of salvation God had for the whole world. Jesus knew the time of His breaking had come. Jesus saw Judas, the Temple guards and the others as messengers come to collect the Bread of Life and distribute Him to the world.

Peter tried to stop those things from happening. He wanted to spare Jesus the pain and humiliation. Jesus rebuked him. When the breaking also propels us into His greater plan, we must recognize and embrace it, rather than trying to escape. Jesus' enemy became His "friend" because the situation helped facilitate His destiny.

Recognize when "Judas" turns up in the storm. There are times to rebuke the devil. There are times to calm the storm.

And there are times to allow God to break us and give us out to others. If you have bound your trouble in prayers, cast it out, fasted and rebuked, confessed the Word and persevered and your circumstances have not changed, look again to see how this trial can make you bread for the hungry. When you cooperate with God's breaking, you can smile at your betrayer, welcome him and call him friend. That does not mean that he will destroy you. Rather, the destructive events in life can become the hidden agenda of God to transform us. In all God is "working together for our good."

At the end of his life Paul wrote, "I am already being poured out as a drink offering." The Lord allows storms that break us with a purpose of knitting us closer to Him. When a lamb or a sheep continually wanders off from the herd, a good shepherd will carefully break its leg. The shepherd then has to carry the lamb until the break is healed. A sheep that spends weeks in the arms of its shepherd, fed out of the shepherd's hand and dependent on him for every need, stays close after that.

The little boy who gave his lunch of bread and some fish to Jesus illustrated something for every Christian. Jesus received the willing offering such as it was with thanks to God. Likewise He receives us as we come in faith. Once we give our lives to Him, they become His to bless and break in order that others may find Christ. The humility, strength, wisdom and peace gained in a right response to suffering will become the food we can offer to others who are struggling to find God.

God will multiply your willingness, faith and talents. He will also use your pain. Jesus told His disciples that day, "You give them something to eat." The stores were closed and, besides, they did not have enough money to buy food for such a large crowd. In Jesus' hands a little lunch offered by a child became more than enough. The twelve baskets the disciples collected were a sign that God would use their service to feed the hungry and that there would never be short supply of His Spirit.

"Come, and let us return to the Lord; for He has torn, but He will heal us; He has stricken, but He will bind us up. After two days He will revive us; on the third day He will raise us up, that we may live in His sight" (Hosea 6:1–2). When our lives are submitted to His purpose and glory, the betrayals, hurts and injustices we experience will become opportunities to cooperate with God's breaking. Like Jesus, we offer ourselves willingly so He can give us away.

The Pain of Glory

Scholars have labored over the hidden mysteries of Jesus' words on Calvary when, clothed in human frailty, He cried out, "God, why have You left me now?" In its simplest meaning, we can see this question as one of common experience. There is hardly an individual alive who has not undergone tribulation without feeling God has deserted him and left him to suffer alone. Jesus experienced that moment when it seemed the heavenly Father had surely turned away. But Jesus took all the punishment required in order that we might have God's perfect peace.

We know the end of the story. Three days after crying out to the Father, Jesus came up out of the grave. Because of our faith in Him our lives are continually sown as a kernel of wheat that must die before it can grow. Every sacrifice will produce a rich harvest. Be certain that God has not left you alone. He still hears us and He still answers—just not necessarily on our timeline. The sense of His power and presence we once experienced may seem to have disappeared, but He is transforming us. We are being changed into His image. To share in His resurrection we must fellowship in His suffering.

The theology of death for first-century Christians was very different from the psychology most people possess today. These believers often suffered and died with joy and courage because of the testimony of Christ. This is why the writer of Hebrews could encourage his hearers not to fear death (see Hebrews 2:15). The fear of death is related to our idea that suffering means rejection by God. It is completely unscriptural to view suffering as a sign that God has deserted us. There is no more poignant example of this throughout history than the existence of the Jewish people. If there is one sign of absolute proof that God does not abandon those who suffer for Him, it is the fact that the Jewish people still live as a race on the earth today and have repossessed in part the ancient land that God promised them thousands of years ago.

The fear of death, along with the attendant inability to deal with suffering, is one reason many Christians are weak in their faith. The New Testament presents death as "falling asleep" or "resting" for a time. The early Church found its commitment and character refined in the fire of persecution, and their ministry laid the foundation on which all of us build.

Micah 7:8 says, "Rejoice not against me, O mine enemy: when I fall, I shall arise; when I sit in darkness, the LORD shall be a light unto me" (KJV). The early Church made a practice of breaking bread together continually and looking after one another's needs. They were broken and persecuted repeatedly. Life must have seemed almost like a continual storm! Yet in the midst of it God gave them a world-shaping, world-changing revival. The breaking process must drive us to our knees in prayer to press us deeper into our relationship with God. As we follow in the footsteps of Christ we are being conformed to His image.

Storms do not seem like setbacks when we have a vision of transformation. Jesus' sacrifice propels us forward to the end of the race with the determination to run for the prize. We will not just stumble over the finish line! We will gird up our loins. We will lift up the hands that hang down. We will make straight paths for our tottering knees and wayward feet, and we will run for the prize. We join our voices with the chorus of those who have gone before us, declaring that the sufferings of this present time are not worthy to be compared with the glory that shall be revealed in us.

Metamorphosis in the Storm

We see then that even the areas of our lives that are dull, brittle and unimpressive contain all the raw materials for the beautiful vision of our Creator. Rather than try to escape the storm, we must allow it to transform us. The fellowship of His suffering may be the vehicle that makes us a testimony of His glory that transforms all who see it. We must allow the extreme conditions to turn our character into something luminous—flexible yet strong.

We might compare the pain, trials, difficulties and opposition in our life work to a butterfly in a cocoon. There is a day coming when we shall be released as beautiful creatures of flight.

Now the cocoon does not come down from God and open up a little door and say, "Come on, caterpillar. Here is your

116

cocoon." No. The caterpillar goes to a certain place at a certain time in its life and begins to clothe itself in its mortality. The silky threads of that new skin begin to harden and shrink. That pressure is the key to its transformation.

The body of the worm is constricted day by day. Everything of its former existence changes dramatically. There is no light, no food, no room for the worm to even move outside the cocoon enshrouding it. In that state, metamorphosis begins.

Under that pressure, the wings are formed. Then begins the worm's struggle to break into the new image of its glory. In that struggle, the wings become functional for flight. As they unfold, the brittle cocoon cracks open, and the new creature emerges.

In Psalm 22:6, after Jesus' cry of dereliction, He continues, "But I am a worm, and no man." He passes through the cocoon of suffering and death and testifies, "You have answered Me!" We see Him afterward, clothed in the glory He possessed before the worlds were made. We must undergo a similar metamorphosis in order to walk in the same image of glory.

Struggle and pain make up the process of transformation from glory to glory. God is working a great redemptive, eternal plan in our lives. He is looking for a people who will offer themselves willingly in the day of His power. We have no guarantees for this temporal life, but we have His eternal precious promises and total provision through the cross. As we lay down our lives for Him, He says, "Not a single hair of your head will be harmed."

The signs of the times seem to indicate that creation is well into the final stages of its struggle. Let us determine in advance that we are storm warriors welcoming the transformation that comes from brokenness.

8

OVERCOMING STORMS IN THE LAST DAYS

And this is the victory that has overcome the world—our faith.

1 John 5:4

Many Christians are confused and troubled by the turbulence they see on the world stage and what these events mean for their lives. The testimony and exhortation of the Bible clears up that confusion: We are in a battle. That may seem like bad news to some, but there is also overwhelming good news: Our Captain Jesus has triumphed! He reigns from the throne in heaven until God makes His enemies His footstool (see Psalm 110:1).

In the meantime we dwell in the tension between "already" and "not yet." The caveat in this battle is that our enemy and God's has not yet conceded his defeat. We must, therefore, hold on to the victory we have been given in the face of Satan's opposition. But resisting evil is not our main focus. We have a strategic mission to carry out. That mission is to proclaim Christ's victory through faithful witness to the Gospel. Our testimony is the vehicle to bring many out of the kingdom of darkness.

In John's Revelation, Jesus says again and again, "He who has an ear, let him hear what the Spirit is saying to the churches." The message we receive has direct effect on the action we take. To put this in military terms, the gathering and dissemination of intelligence is crucial for winning a war. Let's learn how to listen more effectively as the storms erupt more violently in these last days.

God's Positioning System

When a friend gave us a Global Positioning System for our car, we were amazed at the technology. It gives us a constant feed of detailed information, transmitted directly to us from more than two dozen satellites circling the earth. With the touch of a button, we can learn from our GPS where we are and how to get to where we are going. A constantly updated illustrated map indicates our position, and, like something out of an old science fiction film, the GPS speaks to us with a professional woman's voice telling us when to turn and how far to drive on a particular road. If we miss a turn, the system notifies us in that calm voice that it is "recalculating" and maps the next best route to our final destination.

GPS is a dramatic advance in technology for both military and civilian use. If we look at it in comparison to another in-formation-gathering system, sonar, which was developed for military use beginning in World War I, we see a compelling parallel for believers today. A closer look at the contrasts in the two systems shows us the "upgrade" in strategic prophetic accuracy the Holy Spirit is presently giving the Church.

Sonar, an acronym for Sound Navigation and Ranging, makes use of echoes as sound waves bounce between objects in close proximity. Sonar has two modes, passive and active. In the passive mode, technicians listen to nearby sounds. In the active mode, the sonar sends out "pings," pulses of sound energy that travel at the speed of sound in water. As the pings hit an object, some of their energy is reflected back to the receiver and the distance to the object can be determined. The subjective elements of active sonar make it dangerous to use in warfare.

In contrast, GPS uses aerospace technology linking satellites and ground equipment. Global Positioning Systems, which are synchronized with atomic clocks, are not affected by weather but must maintain an unobstructed view of the sky. Satellites transmit three-dimensional data to GPS receivers at the speed of light. The system, maintained by the U.S. Air Force, has drastically changed methods of navigation and is fast becoming important in everyday life.

Thousands of years ago God spoke through Joel, saying that a time would come when the Holy Spirit would be poured out on all flesh. The result would be an advance in readily available knowledge from heaven, being received by men and women at every phase of life.

In the past century there has been a lot of "pinging" going on. As people are filled with the Spirit and begin to exercise spiritual gifts, they give sound to the impulses and impressions they are picking up. But like sonar, a lot of that information is an echo of troubling circumstances and events in close proximity to the persons receiving prophecy. Sometimes the "pings" are even soulish knowledge from personal agendas or obscure—even inaccurate—impressions that mislead many. These short-term impulses coming from untrained or carnal persons not accountable to anyone make the saints vulnerable to enemy plans. Agabus's prophecy to Paul in Acts and Paul's letters to the Corinthians give us much insight into receiving and discerning actionable prophecy.

We are seeing God upgrade the ability of His people to receive and display a more accurate readout of what is coming from heaven. It is His desire that "all may prophesy" and that our prophecy be for the edification, comfort and strengthening of the whole Body of Christ. God's Positioning System is being activated as saints are coming under open heavens in direct reference to His time clock.

More and more we are being trained to recognize true and false prophecy and utilize the real stuff for strategic advances and victories. Intimate knowledge of the Voice of the Lord is activating God's spiritual Air Force and changing lives every day. But we are not seeing just advances in prophecy or the prophetic unction alone. The understanding of what we hear is determined by the way we are trained to receive and serve. This determines the actions we take. As we make ourselves servants of the Holy Spirit and His agenda, our prophecy can be useful, powerful and available to all who are thirsty.

With a dramatic increase of interest in receiving prophetic impressions from the Lord, it has become clear also that the Church is in need of training as to how to understand the impressions we receive. There are three simple guidelines for receiving an upgrade in prophetic accuracy.

1. Apostolic Perspective

The spiritual information coming through dreams, visions and words of spiritual knowledge is only as good as its positive application to the big picture. The mission of the Church is to proclaim the Gospel in power and so advance the Kingdom. Our prophetic contributions should never dilute or distract from the main thing God is doing in an individual's life, a family, a church or a nation.

2. Subjective Authority

GPS is passive. The old-style prophetic was an authoritative voice of religious judgment that was hardly edifying and rarely corrected. The fresh outpouring is a servant spirit open and eager to being evaluated and accountable. This new prophetic posture will keep distraction and confusion to a minimum as many parts coordinate to make up the whole of the revelation we receive.

3. Following Jesus' Style

We notice that Jesus' prophesying was infrequent, concise, practical and accompanied by miracles of healing and deliverance. This is GPS as opposed to sonar. The importance of the prophetic word is to loose the enabling light speed of the anointing for breakthrough. It is to give a clear calculation of where we are on the road to victory in God's plan for our lives and help point the way to the next important intersection with destiny.

Our response to daily events and the constant flood of spiritual "pings" coming from within or from the atmosphere around us must be subject to the big picture coming from the throne. It is this reality that should shape the context of our prophecy and elevate us to the clarity and precision of GPS. God's Positioning System does not just alert us to coming intersections and turns in the road; it also gives us the full picture of our journeys that we might understand the times and know what to do.

When Bonnie told me, Mahesh, to go to Africa as our Aaron was at death's door, I knew she was not hearing according to natural understanding. As we obeyed the directions given by God's Positioning System we were equipped by the Spirit to face the opposition. We overcame our circumstances and became a bridge of overcoming for others.

> Stand therefore, having girded your waist with truth, having put on the breastplate of righteousness, and having shod your feet with the preparation of the gospel of peace; above all, taking the shield of faith with which you will be able to quench all the fiery darts of the wicked one. And take the helmet of salvation, and the sword of the Spirit, which is the word of God; praying always with all prayer and supplication in the Spirit, being watchful to this end with all perseverance and supplication for all the saints.
>
> Ephesians 6:14–18

Effective use of our spiritual armor is predicated upon the first position taken in the heart and mind of the warrior: Stand. Standing indicates the refusal to succumb to difficulty or to placate the enemy by appeasement or retreat. The word *stand* in biblical language is active, not passive. It is not a temporary or arbitrary position. The first response to opposition in the early Church was prayer for boldness to preach and miracles to confirm their testimony (see Acts 4:29–30). They took their signals from heaven and positioned themselves to stand and declare the truth in power.

Watchmen sensitive to the leading of the Holy Spirit are needed now more than ever. We want to be ready for the glory to fall! The Holy Spirit is training the Church to develop a disciplined lifestyle of intercession, fasting, prayer, worship and praise. It may seem like a lot of preparation, but it can mean the difference for people in fulfilling their appointed destinies. In God's set time His glory will fall and all that preparation will pay off.

The new global religion is secular humanism. It promotes confusion and compromise through politically correct tolerance in the name of multiculturalism. Ultimately it enthrones man as God. While rejecting the salvation that only the Lord of glory provides, this false religion is a champion of humanist moralism. Everything from paganism to social justice to environmentalism is going to try to replace the righteousness that can be found only through personal faith in Jesus Christ. If Christians take their direction from the rising pressure of this many-headed world religion, we will be forced into defeat and slavery in one form or another.

Spiritual kingdom is rising against kingdom. We are called to be a clear light shining in the midst of increasing darkness. God wants us to see clearly what is up ahead and prepare effectively to overcome the challenges we face. He is raising up storm warriors who will wage spiritual warfare by gathering supernatural intelligence of what God is up to. As we do so we will be uncovering the enemy's tactics and positions in order to tear down spiritual forces of wickedness in high places.

Following God's Positioning System we will become the instruments of insight and direction to those around us.

How we hear what we hear will determine our destiny in the coming days. As we take the ears of the Spirit and clothe ourselves in the full armor He has availed to us through Calvary, we are positioning ourselves to be overcoming storm warriors.

Intercessors: The "Prayer Force"

We need all parts of the Church Body working together. This is how to keep supplies coming, take care of casualties, train new recruits and send out a new wave of frontline warriors. Our combat theater is the world, for God is sending His soldiers into all nations to see the Kingdom of God manifest in its fullness.

Strategic intercession is a key component of this battle. We liken it to a "prayer force"! The prayers of the intercessors storm the heavens—combating the strategies of the enemy once the troops are moving on the ground.

I, Bonnie, will never forget a particular night in Kinshasa, Zaire, during one of our outreaches in the region. The needs were massive. Multitudes were coming every night to hear the Gospel, but our team consisted of Mahesh, myself, one other American and a handful of African pastors. We were already stretched to the maximum of our capacity when Mahesh came down with malaria. We needed some major reinforcements.

At home we had a committed group of praying supporters. They came together every week to spend time in worship and to pray for us. I knew that we needed their prayers now more than ever, but from our remote location in the bush there was no telephone connection to enable me to communicate our situation to anyone in the outside world. I prayed the Lord would break through with His miracles, and then crawled into bed, exhausted. It seemed I had just fallen asleep when I was awakened by voices. I opened my eyes in the darkness and recognized the familiar sound of several of our intercessors. I was awestruck, as it seemed they were marching up and down praying in the Spirit right there in the room! The Holy Spirit had alerted our prayer force!

Gratitude, comfort and assurance flooded my soul as I realized there was no distance between us and them in the Spirit. They had gathered in spiritual battle formation and were providing effective "air cover" against the attack we faced. They were breaking through for our victory and successful completion of that mission to bring thousands of souls into the Kingdom. Tears came to my eyes as I heard them lifting up our need before the throne of our Father in heaven. We were not alone in this battle.

We needed the help of our "prayer force" in order to complete the mission on which God had sent us. These combatants were armed and ready. They had a history of prayer with God. They had been trained and discipled as they participated in corporate prayer together, and they had added to their arsenal with regular fasting to boost the power of their intercessions. When the time came that we needed their reinforcements, they were prepared.

The prayers of those warriors brought the breakthrough. God answered. Mahesh awoke on the mend and was back preaching by evening as our faithful intercessors launched war from the heavenlies, bringing relief for us on the ground.

Intercession on an even larger scale becomes one of the most powerful weapons in the Lord's arsenal. This is the corporate watch, during which individuals are discipled in the glory and harmonize in prayer. The atomic power of corporate fasting and prayer in combination with the strategic intelligence gathered in this setting knocks out the strongmen and paralyzes the enemy, setting people and nations free.

Every Friday night for more than a dozen years our church's congregation has kept watch all night. This discipline is intermittently an intense time of warfare and a joyful date night with Jesus. The secret of success in keeping the watch is to *keep doing it together*! Many nights it is simply a matter of perseverance—just showing up to watch and pray. Then there are key moments when God downloads strategic insight and our prayers have major impact on the lives of those who gather together to worship and on our world.

We have played strategic roles in many recorded successes for the Kingdom of God—from terrorist plots being uncovered in our own nation and abroad to the rise and fall of powerful politicians to salvation for the loved ones of families participating in the watch service. This training ground has produced a many-membered team of powerful storm warriors equipped to know the times and seasons and understand what to do.

In the battles we face in this day and age there are no casual observers. The luxury of remaining neutral or uninvolved in the storm is not ours to take. In fact, inaction can be just as deadly as the assault of the enemy's forces. The battle is not "out there" somewhere on a foreign field; it is right in our midst. The first battlefront is in our hearts as we determine to tune our ears to heaven and set our sights on His Kingdom glory in everything we say and do.

"V" Is for Victory

I, Mahesh, love to go goose hunting. In studying the habits of these amazing creatures, I have learned another important lesson about the last days' battle between spiritual kingdoms. By instinct geese fly the squadron formation of a V. That pattern is the secret to their ability to travel across whole continents when they are on the move.

Scientists have long theorized as to why geese and other large migratory birds adopt this formation. A certain team of scientists found at least one answer: By taping heart monitors to pelicans that were trained to fly behind a small airplane, they proved that it actually makes for more efficient flying. The heart rates of the birds flying in a V were lower than when flying solo. The birds used less energy and burned less body fuel when traveling as a company than when flying alone. They could glide more often in formation, and faced less air resistance.

In addition, in a V formation each bird has an unobstructed field of vision, allowing flock members to communicate while in flight. Jet fighter pilots use this formation for the same reason. The goose at the head of the V is not necessarily the leader of the flock; the geese take turns leading. As one bird tires it drops back and another takes its place.

A flock of geese can fly 70 percent farther by adopting the V shape! Now that is what we call teamwork.

This is a good illustration of the importance of moving together in the power of the Holy Spirit. As we let God group us into spiritual families, we will be more effective overcomers than we might be on our own. The faith of each believer added to a team of others will give us the same kind of advantage the V formation gives birds in flight.

There is an exciting war story about a group of prisoners that also illustrates the power of teamwork. These men overcame their captivity together through patience and persistence.

During World War II, 76 Allied soldiers escaped from a high-security Nazi prison camp before their tunnel was discovered. It became known as the "Great Escape." Six hundred men worked around the clock for more than a year to accomplish their mission. They engineered and dug an elaborate set of tunnels. The dirt was extracted by teaspoonfuls and ferried out of the tunnels onto the camp yard through pockets sewn into the men's prison uniforms. They secured and constructed lighting in the tunnels and built a special bellows to force fresh air in for those who were digging the shafts.

The prisoners even created "escape suits" so they would not be seen in prison garb once they were outside the prison camp. Men who were talented in handwriting, languages and printing were put to work forging identification and travel documents for the escapees. They worked in shifts in order to maintain the appearance of "life as usual" in the prison camp.

The entire project required more than 4,000 bed slats, 1,699 blankets, 52 long tables, 1,219 knives, 30 shovels, 600 feet of rope and 1,000 feet of electric wire. All of these had to be stolen under the scrutiny and abuse of the camp guards and officials. Loyalty, commitment, secrecy and discipline were maintained for months in spite of their severe personal conditions. The Great Escape is an inspiring true story, showing how people can harmonize together to accomplish the impossible.

God is calling His end time army out in formation. Every person's faith and cooperation is absolutely necessary. We need one another's gifts in order to complete the mission God has for our generation. It is not sufficient anymore to say, "I'll support your program if you support mine." Like the POWs who linked their destinies and submitted themselves to the plan of escape for the whole company, we need to allow the Lordship of the Holy Spirit to unite us and plant us in the place He has ordained for service. There every person is in position for fresh anointing and new and powerful manifestations of the gifts of the Spirit in their lives. Individualism will not contribute to victory.

The Holy Spirit is restoring the fivefold ministry of Ephesians 4:11—apostles, prophets, evangelists, pastors and teachers—to the Church. These offices are appointed by the Lord to "equip" the saints for ministry. The Greek word used by Paul to describe these persons literally means "to set in order," in the manner of a surgeon resetting a broken bone. Working together under the headship of the Holy Spirit, Jesus is restoring rank and order, authority and demonstration of His power through His Church to the world. It is time to "lay aside every weight, and the sin which so easily ensnares us, and let us run with endurance the race that is set before us" (Hebrews 12:1). God is calling us up higher so that together we might lay hold of the prize of our high calling: to overcome the world!

Keep Striking

Scripture says that our enemy the devil is roaming around like a roaring lion seeking whom he may devour. Our objectives in the Kingdom, therefore, must remain clear and uncompromising. We must each develop and maintain a disposition of persistence in the face of all odds. It begins at the level of personal daily discipline and extends to full collaboration in the Body. We must look beyond personal victory to a vision of corporate accountability. We must never give up and never give in to any other vision. We must complete the mission. All it takes is a company of warriors who are trained, obedient to God, willing to sacrifice and fearless in the face of evil.

> Therefore do not cast away your confidence, which has great reward. For you have need of endurance, so that after you have done the will of God, you may receive the promise: "For yet a little while, and He who is coming will come and will not tarry. Now the just shall live by faith; but if anyone draws back, My soul has no pleasure in him." But we are not of those who draw back to perdition, but of those who believe to the saving of the soul.
>
> Hebrews 10:35–39

There are major challenges up ahead. We have passed the point of no return on the prophetic time clock that is ticking down to Christ's appearing. Our ultimate assurance for victory in this battle is simple: Never give in.

Our Champion overcame by taking His stand on the side of the Father's will. Once He positioned Himself, no one could move Him away from that determination. Not the devil. Not friends, faithful and unfaithful. Not temptation, suffering and, finally, not even death itself. His ultimate weapon was simple perseverance. He told the saints through John, "Hold fast what you have, that no one may take your crown" (Revelation 3:11). His exhortation is for us today.

We have three advantages already. There are three powerful weapons guaranteeing victory: (1) the blood of the Lamb cleanses and sets us free from condemnation and death; (2) the testimony of our personal faith in the Lamb speaks louder than the wisdom of human philosophy and false religion; and (3) we are assured that death ultimately has no hold on us because the Lamb who was dead is alive forever. These truths position us to reach our destination: eternal life and reward in God's presence. This is the victory.

9

AUTHORITY OVER THE
DEMONIC STORM

"But if I cast out demons by the Spirit of God, surely the kingdom of God has come upon you."

Matthew 12:28

When I, Mahesh, was a graduate student in Lubbock, Texas, I received a clear word from God to go to Dallas on a specific weekend. I did not know exactly what God had in mind. I knew that a conference was being held there, so I called a friend who lived in the area to see if I could stay with him, and drove to Dallas.

For three days I attended the conference faithfully, which was the only reason that I could think of for God asking me to come. Nothing remarkable happened. I did discover that my friend's life was in shambles. His wife had just left him and he was trying to raise their two young children by himself. I thought that perhaps God had brought me there to witness to him, but every time I started to say something, the Lord stopped me. I began to wonder if I had really heard the Lord at all. As a graduate student, I had limited funds and scarce time to spare. It seemed on the surface that I had just wasted a perfectly good weekend.

On my last day in town, my friend and I were invited to dinner at the home of the woman who watched his children during the day. As we drove to their house, I again asked the Lord if I was to witness to him. Once more the answer was no. Still wondering why I had come all this distance, we turned onto the woman's street and drove into what looked like a scene from a horror movie.

The woman was standing in her front yard holding my friend's blood-covered toddler in her arms. She was pointing toward the backyard and screaming hysterically, "He's killing my husband! He's killing my husband!" At the sight of his little daughter, my friend went into such a panic that I had to leave him in the front yard with the woman while I went in search of the husband.

My heart pounding with adrenaline, I ran toward the backyard. Rounding the corner of the house, I saw the largest German shepherd I have ever seen mauling her husband. Blood was everywhere. The dog had apparently attacked the child, and when the man had come to her rescue, the dog had turned on him. The vicious attack had severed major blood vessels. The man collapsed on the ground as I came upon the scene.

At that moment the Holy Spirit said to me, *This is why I sent you.* The crazed dog looked up and eyed me as I received this commission from the Lord.

Thank you very much! I thought. I looked around for anything to defend myself and grabbed the nearest items at hand: a plastic lawn chair and a flimsy broom. With my heart in my throat, I wielded my ridiculous weapons and started to approach the dog. He was growling and baring his teeth and ready to pounce when I heard the Lord say, *Bind it.*

I was just learning the things of the Spirit and I thought, *Bind it? I don't have any rope.* Then the dog leapt at me, and I suddenly had a revelation of what the Lord meant. "I bind you in the name of Jesus!" I cried. The dog hit an invisible wall and fell backward onto the ground. He lay there whimpering and cowering as I ran to the man's side.

We called an ambulance, but the man had lost so much blood that he stopped breathing and died before they arrived. Sitting beside him I thought, *Lord, I know You didn't bring me all the way here to watch this man die.* I put my hand on his chest and said, "In Jesus' name, breath come back." Joined by my friend with his daughter, I sat there praying for what seemed like minutes. Suddenly the man gave a loud sigh and came to life again.

My host and I jumped into the ambulance to ride with the man to the hospital. Once inside, I saw both men staring at me in disbelief. One had been brought back from the dead, and the other had just witnessed his resurrection! The whole family was delivered that day.

Now lead them to Me, I heard God instruct me. As you can imagine, it was easy for them to accept Jesus, having seen His authority in the midst of a demonic storm.

My encounter that day was my first experience of the absolute authority that we have in the name of Jesus over every power in the demonic realm. It is a lesson that I will never forget, and it is a dramatic illustration for each of us as we face the opposition and destructive force of the enemy of our souls.

Foundations for Deliverance

Many of us face the storms of demonic oppression. Failure to understand our authority in the name of Jesus leaves us powerless to free ourselves and others. We may see the fierce bite of the enemy and feel unable to act. But Jesus has commissioned each of us to tear down these strongholds and loose the captives: "All authority has been given to Me in heaven and on earth. Go therefore and make disciples of all the nations" (Matthew 28:18–19).

God has called each of us to be carriers of His glory for the salvation and deliverance of many. While the influence of demons is not always as dramatically apparent as the devastating attack on the man in this story, Satan has no less deadly an agenda for all those he oppresses day to day. Strongholds, curses and areas of dark oppression are in his arsenal. But Jesus is much greater than Satan! As we have stated before, Scripture proclaims that greater is He who is in us than he who is in the world. God has given us His anointing and authority to disarm the demonic realm of its power over individuals, cities and nations so His Kingdom might advance against the kingdom of darkness.

Deliverance from demons is, in fact, a manifestation of the advance of God's Kingdom. No one before Jesus wielded this kind of authority. Moses, Elijah and all the prophets did many signs and wonders, but there is not one record of them casting out demons. The religious leaders of Jesus' day said, "What is this? What new doctrine is this? For with authority He commands even the unclean

138

spirits, and they obey Him" (Mark 1:27). Deliverance was the evidence that Christ was greater than all who came before Him. His Kingdom is not in words. His Kingdom is in power. One way that power is demonstrated is deliverance from demons.

Jesus never separated the ministry of deliverance from the preaching of the Gospel. In Mark 1:39 we read that Jesus "was preaching in their synagogues throughout all Galilee, and casting out demons." When He sent out His disciples, "He called the twelve to Himself, and began to send them out two by two, and gave them power over unclean spirits" (Mark 6:7). Jesus demonstrated deliverance as central to the message of the Gospel. He said, "Go into all the world and preach the gospel to every creature. . . . And these signs will follow those who believe: In My name they will cast out demons" (Mark 16:15, 17).

Jesus delivered regular men and women, those who lived their lives in obedience to the Scriptures. As Derek Prince used to say, "You don't have to be a pervert, a criminal or a lunatic to need deliverance from demons." In Matthew 8:16, for instance, we read that many observant Jews waited until after sunset so as not to break the Sabbath in seeking Jesus' ministry: "When evening had come, they brought to Him many who were demon-possessed. And He cast out the spirits with a word, and healed all who were sick."

After His resurrection Jesus commissioned all who believe to preach the Gospel with signs following; the very first sign He mentions is authority to cast out demons. It is still the primary job description of every believer. Jesus went about doing the work the Father had given Him to do. He said that we would do the works that He did, and also greater works than these. Christians have been given authority to bring deliverance and bind the work of the enemy.

The Nature of Demons

Satan is a fallen archangel, and demons are an order of lesser spirits he directs to oppress, torment and oppose mankind. The Greek words used to denote demons in Scripture are *diamon* or *diamonion*. These same words were used by the pagan religions of that day to refer to divine or semi-divine spirits. Many of the pagan rituals and cultic practices common to the Greek and the Roman cultures sought to appropriate these spirits for their own welfare or purposes. The Bible also refers to demons as evil or unclean spirits.

Scripture uses two different Greek expressions to describe the influence of these spirits on the lives of men. One is *to have* a demon. This is the expression used in Matthew 11:18: "For John came neither eating nor drinking, and they say, 'He has a demon.'" The other is *to be under the influence of* a demon. This is the form used to describe the man delivered from a legion of demons in the country of the Gadarenes in Mark 5:1–20.

Unlike fallen angels, which have bodies and inhabit the heavenlies, demons are earthbound spirits without bodies. This is why they have an intense craving to inhabit a body through which they can act out their evil desires.

"When an unclean spirit goes out of a man, he goes through dry places, seeking rest, and finds none. Then he says, 'I will return to my house from which I came.' And when he comes, he finds it empty, swept, and put in order. Then he goes and takes with him seven other spirits more wicked than himself, and they enter and dwell there."

Matthew 12:43–45

Demons have personalities. They have an express will, emotions, knowledge, self-awareness and the ability to speak. Their primary assignment from Satan is to keep us from salvation. Failing that, their second assignment is to keep believers from serving the Lord effectively and advancing the Kingdom. Thirdly they torment and oppress people wherever they are allowed.

Demons typically use the same strategies over and over again. They will entice, harass, torment, compel, drive, en-slave, defile, deceive, weaken physically and cause infirmity or disease. Demons will try to gain entrance to our lives or influence over us through our emotions, attitudes, relation-ships, thoughts, tongues, sexuality, addictions and physical infirmities. Demonic oppression and physical infirmity fre-quently work together to create a stronghold that hinders our effective service to the Lord and His Kingdom. This is why healing often accompanied deliverance from evil spirits in Jesus' ministry.

The primary indication of demonic activity is an attack on our peace. Restlessness is a hallmark of demonic pres-ence. When distracting thoughts, impulses, nervousness or compulsions become principal influences over someone, demonic activity is present. An extreme example of this is obsessive-compulsive disorder.

When demons operate externally we can resist them. If we experience them internally we must cast them out. You will find that demonic oppression comes to the surface in the atmosphere of the anointing. When demons encountered

Jesus as He preached in Galilee, they were stirred up and cried out, revealing their presence.

Second Kings 6:5–7 records the story of the iron axe head that floated to the surface of the river when Elisha put a rod in the water. The anointing that resided in Elisha drew up the hidden object to the surface so that it could be retrieved. In the same way the anointing will bring demonic activity to the surface so that deliverance can come. In the vibration of the anointing, demonic strongholds will begin to shake loose from their moorings and be manifest. The anointing of the Holy Spirit will break yokes.

The Good News: Deliverance Can Be Yours

There are two main reasons for the corrupt human condition: flesh and demons. Flesh is the old fallen nature of sin that we inherited from our ancestors and have contributed to through our own actions and attitudes. The struggle with sin and our fallen nature is a universal problem. Demons, on the other hand, do not necessarily affect everyone.

While the symptoms of both may look similar, the remedies are different. For the flesh, it is the cross. For demons, it is deliverance. You cannot cast out the flesh and you cannot crucify a demon! We expel demons by the authority of Jesus' name, and we walk out our deliverance by dying daily to our fleshly passions and desires in order to keep our house swept clean and fully inhabited by the Holy Spirit.

If you have repeatedly confessed and repented of a sin, but find yourself falling into the same pattern no matter how hard you resist and fight against it, this is often the indication that there is demonic influence holding you back from the fullness of victory. Other indications may be chronic oppression of your physical, emotional or spiritual well-being that you can never quite overcome despite regular fasting, prayer, ministry and reading the Word of God. The solution is simple: deliverance.

Jesus cast out demons with a word. It is the Holy Spirit who drives away demons and establishes the peace of Christ's Kingdom over us and our households. Where the Spirit of the Lord is, there is liberty.

We receive and minister deliverance in seven simple steps.

1. Humble Ourselves

Humility is the door by which we welcome the ministry of the Holy Spirit for deliverance. Acknowledging our need for His power and intervention will align our hearts for Him to work in us unhindered by pride or fear.

2. Be Completely Honest

Being frank with ourselves and the Lord regarding the areas into which we have fallen and need His delivering power is vital to receiving freedom. We allow the Lord to get to the root of our problems by letting go of all the trappings that we may have used to disguise our sin. We must call a spade a spade.

3. Confess Our Sins

First John 1:9 states, "If we confess our sins, He is faithful and just to forgive us our sins and to cleanse us from all unrighteousness." Confessing our sins to the Lord removes the legal foothold for a demon to claim any place in our lives. Anyone dealing with a major stronghold may find it helpful to confess to church leaders as well.

4. Repent and Renounce

Repentance is a change of mind. We make a conscious decision to turn from our sins and old patterns. It is essential to renounce any involvement with the occult and false religions including idolatry, witchcraft, sorcery and related dark practices. We must break all ties related to these evils.

5. Forgive

"And whenever you stand praying, if you have anything against anyone, forgive him, that your Father in heaven may also forgive you your trespasses. But if you do not forgive, neither will your Father in heaven forgive your trespasses" (Mark 11:25–26). Unforgiveness is a prison that will hold us in captivity. When we offer forgiveness, the prison door opens for us to be released.

6. Call on the Name of the Lord

"Whosoever shall call on the name of the LORD shall be delivered" (Joel 2:32, KJV). We cast out demons in the name of Jesus. There is no demonic power that can resist His name. When we have submitted ourselves to His Lordship, we walk in the authority of His name over every demonic hold.

This is one of the distinctions between the flesh and demonic oppression. Demons cannot resist His name, but the flesh can. If the "demon" is not responding to the authority of the name of Jesus, it is a strong indication that the issue we are dealing with is the sin nature of our flesh. Romans 8:13

instructs us, "If you live according to the flesh you will die; but if by the Spirit you put to death the deeds of the body, you will live." The only remedy for our flesh is to crucify it through daily repentance and self-discipline.

7. Cast Out the Demon

"In My name they will cast out demons" (Mark 16:17). After praying for deliverance in the name of Jesus, we simply cast out the demons. We encourage people to breathe out as they are going through deliverance, as demons will often come out through the mouth. Yawning, sighing, a tickling in your nose, fire or heat in your body, tears or vomiting may all be manifestations of deliverance. Manifestations are not necessary for a person to receive deliverance, however. Demons will frequently leave without any physical sensation at all.

Here is a prayer that you may wish to use as a basis for deliverance.

Lord Jesus Christ, Your name is above every other name, and I declare that You are Lord of my heart and my life. Father, I confess my sins of . . . and I turn from them. Lord Jesus, You took every infirmity and every area of darkness to the cross for me, and Your blood has the power to set me free. I apply it now. I plead the blood of Jesus over every area of my life. Lord, I forgive those who have offended me and release them and any anger, unforgiveness and bitterness to You now, in Jesus' name. My body is a temple of the Holy Spirit, and I invite You, Holy Spirit, to fill me, body, soul and spirit. Father in heaven, I renounce every contact that I have had with any and every form of sorcery, witchcraft, false religion and the occult. I renounce all sins of the flesh. Lord Jesus, in Your name, through Your blood, I command every evil spirit, demonic oppression or influence that has tormented, harassed, enslaved or compelled me to go now. Father, by the power of the Holy Spirit, sweep this house of mine clean in the name of Jesus Christ. Amen.

The fruit of deliverance from demons is joy! Public rejoicing, thanksgiving and testimony are all biblical responses to deliverance. If you have experienced deliverance, begin thanking the Lord. Praise His name and rejoice that He is the King with authority over every power of darkness, and that He has set you free!

Seven Ways to Stay "Demon Free"

Deliverance from demons is a complete work, finished by the authority and power of Jesus' name. We see, however, from Jesus' temptation in the wilderness and His description of the unclean spirit in Matthew 12:44, that the devil and his demons will look for an opportune time to return. There are seven basic disciplines that build up our defenses and close the doors to the return of demonic oppression.

1. Submit to the Lordship of Jesus

Blatant rebellion to the Lordship of Jesus in any area of our lives is an open door of invitation to the demonic realm. Repentance and submission to His Word and authority is necessary to stay delivered from demons.

2. Be Filled Continually with the Holy Spirit

Luke 11:13 says: "If you then, being evil, know how to give good gifts to your children, how much more will your heavenly Father give the Holy Spirit to those who ask Him!" The Holy Spirit is the promised gift of the Father to everyone who believes. Once our "home" has been vacated of demons, cultivating our relationship with the Holy Spirit through ongoing communion, speaking in tongues and singing in the Spirit will keep our "inner man" filled, leaving no place for the enemy to return.

3. Live by the Word of God

"[My words] are life to those who find them, and health to all their flesh" (Proverbs 4:22). When Jesus was tempted in the wilderness, He resisted every assault, deception and strategy of Satan with the Word of God. Disciplining ourselves to spend time learning and storing the Word of God in our hearts and aligning our beliefs and our actions to its instruction will guard us from the snare of the devil.

4. Put on the Whole Armor of God

Paul instructs us to put on the whole armor of God that we might withstand the "wiles of the devil" (Ephesians 6:11). Daily attention to our spiritual armor and a heart full of the joy of our salvation expressed in thanksgiving and praise are keys to living a demon-free life.

5. Cultivate Right Relationships

Choosing whom we relate to and how we do it has an impact on our outlook, attitude, lifestyle and ultimately our freedom from oppression. As we mentioned earlier, relationships can be one of the areas where we will be tested and tried in walking out our deliverance. Our relationships with those with whom we have a history of conflict or sin need to be brought into discipline as we align our flesh to the reality of our deliverance from oppression. We do this by choosing to react and relate differently in relationships where we previously had strongholds of sin, anger, manipulation, bitterness, rejection and the like. Removing ourselves from relationships and activities that would pull us back into the darkness from which we have escaped is an important step in keeping our deliverance.

6. Cultivate Right Fellowship

Fellowship was one of the main activities of the early Church. It was central to effective discipleship of new believers, the teaching of the Word and the apostles' doctrine, prayer and the communion of the saints. Surrounding ourselves in fellowship with believers will encourage, disciple, teach, edify us in our faith and strengthen our spiritual walls and defenses against the enemy's attack. Right fellowship and submission to the authorities He has put in our lives will protect, heal and build up the broken places that originally made us susceptible to demons.

7. Make Jesus Central

Jesus is our model and means for living a demon-free life. Scripture tells us that the devil found no place in Him (see John 14:30). His words to all who would follow Him are this: "If anyone desires to come after Me, let him deny himself, and take up his cross, and follow Me. For whoever desires to save his life will lose it, but whoever loses his life for My sake will find it" (Matthew 16:24–25). Jesus' heart was set on the will of His Father, even to the point of death on the cross. As we follow in His footsteps, dying to ourselves and our old corrupt nature through obedience and submission to His will, we will overcome every demonic attack by His blood, by our testimony and the fact that we do not love our own lives even unto death.

Curses: A Doorway for Oppression

Another avenue of oppression in people's lives is curses. The power of a curse is different from demonic harassment because it takes hold through deliberate disobedience or rejection of the principles in the Word of God. In other words, sinning, missing the mark, can open the way to demonic harassment. Purposely defying the Word of God opens the way for demons to gain a stronger hold through a curse. Idolatry, treachery toward the innocent and anti-Semitism are three primary ways curses can come.

Scripture tells us that a curse without a cause cannot alight. If you see the effects of a curse in your life but have truly repented of all known sins, you may be suffering the effects of sin in a previous generation of your family line. It is possible for a curse and its attendant demons to come down through generational lines if one's forebears were involved in iniquitous activities. Chronic or recurring disease, accidents, premature death and poverty can all be the effects of a family-line curse. Ongoing failure and resistance to blessing, when one has done all one can to obey God and His Word, might be evidence of a curse at work. A sense of deadness or deathlike symptoms—in contrast to life and revival—can also be the indicator of a curse.

Dealing with curses is much the same as casting out demons, although it requires specific repentance on the part of those who are affected—either for their own sins or the sins of their ancestors. Renunciation of the sin and cleansing by the power of the blood will negate the hold and effect of a curse. A simple prayer in the name of Jesus under the anointing will break it.

Galatians 3:13–14 tells us:

> Christ has redeemed us from the curse of the law, having become a curse for us (for it is written, "Cursed is everyone who hangs on a tree"), that the blessing of Abraham might come upon the Gentiles in Christ Jesus, that we might receive the promise of the Spirit through faith.

Jesus has made a way for every curse to be broken, becoming the curse for us on the cross. The opposite of a curse is experiencing the blessing of God. He wants each of us to be free from curses so that we might experience the fullness of the blessings He intends to rest on our family and on every area of our lives.

One Drop of Blood

The foundation for our deliverance is Jesus and Jesus only. We are simply His "superconductors" for the power of His Spirit and glory to flow through. Jesus is advancing His Kingdom. Be it one demon or a legion, Jesus will cause the enemy to flee. He is stronger than any demonic principality. "Having disarmed principalities and powers, [Jesus] made a public spectacle of them, triumphing over them in [the cross]" (Colossians 2:15). Jesus overpowers the strongman, takes away his armor and divides up the spoils. He has transferred this authority to His Church so we can set free all those who are bound.

During one of our evangelistic outreaches in Africa, the Lord woke me, Mahesh, one morning to tell me He would do a mass deliverance that day. My immediate response was, "Lord, where are my helpers?" The crowds at these meetings numbered up to two hundred thousand people, stretching into the darkness as far as the eye could see. These were people steeped in all kinds of sorcery and false religion. They were in bondage to sin, disease and oppression. I was just one little evangelist with an interpreter and half a dozen African pastors to help me who did not speak the same language. And God was asking me to do a mass deliverance service!

The Lord answered, *Mahesh, I said we are going to do a mass deliverance service. I AM the helper.*

When I arrived at the meeting that evening, a terrified committee of the local pastors met me. More than eight hundred sorcerers from all over the region had come to loose curses on us, but the Holy Spirit downloaded a revelation I had never experienced before.

That night 150,000 people were in attendance. During my preaching I saw, by the Spirit, the true power that rests in the blood of Calvary. I proclaimed, "One drop of the blood of Jesus Christ can destroy the kingdom of Satan!" When I made that declaration under the anointing, the Lord broke the power of witchcraft and demonic oppression over the crowd. People writhed and screamed as demons left them. Sick and maimed bodies were instantaneously made whole. The night air was filled with loud crying and wailing as the power for deliverance was loosed. The witch doctors no longer had their power. Thousands of people gave their hearts to Jesus and received eternal life.

When the Lord was finished with His work, a hush settled over the crowd, and the peace of God's presence and healing filled the atmosphere.

Pulling Down Strongholds

Strongmen and territorial spirits are under the direction of Satan, occupying a higher level than demons in the spiritual realms. We can use the analogy from J. R. R. Tolkien's *The Lord of the Rings* to get a mental picture of this hierarchy.

Tolkien created creatures he called Nazguls, evil, dark beings who commanded thousands of lesser dark minions called orcs. In the kingdom of darkness the "princes" are strongmen like Tolkien's Nazguls. They hold sway over a territory and command demons as their infantry. The activity of this dark hierarchy creates a stronghold. Strongmen have armor, weapons and power to oppress and blind the people under their domain, creating an atmosphere over a region, in a family or in an individual's life that resists the knowledge of Jesus Christ. While the oppression may manifest in blatant violence, poverty or witchcraft, these conditions are secondary to the main objective of the stronghold: to blind the people to obedience to Jesus Christ.

The strongman is like the general of an army. When the general is taken captive, the battle is essentially won. When the strongman is bound through prayer, the Kingdom can advance and the blessings of God can begin to be realized. God's ground troops can go in with the Gospel, bringing salvation, healing and deliverance. The name of Jesus and the delivering power of His blood are supreme. When two or more of His saints join ranks in spiritual battle formation through prayer, we can rout the strongest enemies of the Kingdom of God.

This magnifies the importance of corporate prayer. We can change cultures and transform families, societies and whole nations as we learn to identify and tear down strongholds, taking them captive to the knowledge and obedience of Jesus.

Early in my ministry I, Mahesh, was invited to hold evangelistic services in a small town in New Mexico. The pastor who had invited me warned, "We have not had a salvation in our city for several years." People simply did not get saved in that city. Other than Christians who migrated there from other towns, church growth was stagnant and the congregations were aging.

I did not know what to make of this. I was still young in the Lord and I was learning about spiritual warfare. I asked the Lord, "What is this?"

He said, *It's not complicated. There is a territorial spirit over that region. Take authority over it.*

I said, "Yes, sir!" In the weeks before my meetings, I began to fast and pray and take authority over the stronghold that the Lord had shown me.

During the series of meetings I held there, the Lord did some of the most amazing miracles I have ever seen. I found that not only had the region been under a cloud preventing people from coming to the Lord, but the cloud had shut down all manifestations of God's miraculous power. Now that the strongman was bound, the Lord was using me to plunder the territory. Seventy-six people gave their lives to the Lord on the first night alone! We experienced breakthrough because the Lord had shown us the strongman and given us the authority to bind that power and see many come to salvation.

For the weapons of our warfare are not carnal but mighty in God for pulling down strongholds, casting down arguments and every high thing that exalts itself against the knowledge of God, bringing every thought into captivity to the obedience of Christ.

2 Corinthians 10:4–5

Here are seven weapons that are mighty in God for pulling down strongholds.

1. The Name of Jesus

Personal revelation of the name above every other name gives us authority to bind the strongman.

2. The Blood of Jesus

Revelation 12:11 says, "And they overcame him by the blood of the Lamb." This is one of our most powerful weapons against the enemy.

3. Discernment

First Corinthians 12:7–8, 10 says, "The manifestation of the Spirit is given to each one for the profit of all: for to one is given the word of wisdom through the Spirit . . . to another discerning of spirits." Discernment is a gift that comes by the power of the Holy Spirit to reveal the name of the strongman. Ask the Lord to show you the spiritual force to target in your prayer.

4. The Armor of God

Ephesians 6:13 tells us, "Therefore take up the whole armor of God, that you may be able to withstand in the evil day, and having done all, to stand." The armor of God is the basic equipment needed to stand in the battle. These are defensive and aggressive weapons: His truth, His righteousness, the Gospel, faith, salvation and the Word. These will protect and advance us against the assault of the enemy.

5. Prayer

In Matthew 18:18–20, Jesus states,

"Whatever you bind on earth will be bound in heaven, and whatever you loose on earth will be loosed in heaven. Again I say to you that if two of you agree on earth concerning anything that they ask, it will be done for them by My Father in heaven. For where two or three are gathered together in My name, I am there in the midst of them."

As we mentioned in chapter 8, aggressive prayer is intensified through corporate watching and fasting. Corporate prayer is an essential end time weapon as we advance the Kingdom against the ancient strongholds of the antichrist spirit over nations and regions opposed to the Gospel.

6. Praise

In 2 Chronicles 20:22 we read, "Now when they began to sing and to praise, the LORD set ambushes against the people of Ammon, Moab, and Mount Seir, who had come against Judah; and they were defeated." Praise is a launching place for the weapons of victory over the strongholds of the enemy.

7. Proclamation

Revelation 12:11, quoted above, says further, "And they overcame him by . . . the word of their testimony." Mighty miracles are loosed when we declare the supernatural works of the Lord. The testimony of what He has done is a powerful weapon for disarming the enemy.

Take the Spoils

Jesus said, "When a strong man, fully armed, guards his own palace, his goods are in peace. But when a stronger than he comes upon him and overcomes him, he takes from him all his armor in which he trusted, and divides his spoils" (Luke 11:21–22).

My family was descended from Rajputs, the warrior cast of India. We could trace back my Hindu ancestry by name for eight hundred years. To my knowledge not one person in my family line had ever believed in Jesus Christ. They were all Hindus. They took pride in their Hinduism. As a boy growing up I was told, "Your ancestors have died fighting for the faith. You must also be a warrior for Hinduism."

But when I was sixteen, I read the New Testament and came to know Jesus as my personal Savior. I was able to lead one of my sisters to the Lord shortly after. But year after year I kept praying for the rest of my family without any breakthrough in the shroud of Hinduism that surrounded them.

I had been serving the Lord for years and seen many come to salvation, but my family remained unmoved. I prayed, "Lord, You are saving thousands of people, healing and delivering them as I take Your Gospel to the nations, but what about my family? Lord, I want my mother and my sisters to be saved. I want my brother to be saved. Lord, I love my family so much and I want them to know You."

The Lord answered by showing me that there was a stronghold over my family that was preventing them from hearing and receiving the message of the Gospel. When I began to pray to bind the power of that strongman with fasting, the breakthrough came. I led my entire family to receive the Lord. They were born again and delivered from their spiritual oppression. My sister was healed instantly of a chronic infirmity that had plagued her for years. All of them were radically changed. They shared their new knowledge with others. Their past history and traditions of Hinduism and idolatry were wiped away by the power of the blood of Jesus.

God wants us to possess His promises, but strongholds will undoubtedly stand in the way, whether they be over our family, our church or our nation. When Moses sent the spies into the land of Canaan to scout out the land of their inheritance, they returned with this report: "We went to the land where you sent us. It truly flows with milk and honey, and this is its fruit. Nevertheless the people who dwell in the land are strong; the cities are fortified and very large; moreover we saw the descendants of Anak there" (Numbers 13:27–28).

Ten of the twelve spies whom Moses sent into the land were affected by the strongholds of the region. They saw that the promises of the Lord were true, the land *was* a land of milk and honey just as He had said, but they came under the influence of the spiritual strongholds. Their minds were taken captive so that their beliefs, thoughts and imagination could see only defeat. Only Joshua and Caleb, who had "a different spirit" (Numbers 14:24), held on to God's promise and believed that they should go up and possess their inheritance. We have been given a different spirit, the promised Holy Spirit. He dwells in us and works through us to break the power of the enemy. Nothing is impossible with God.

You may be experiencing a drought in your family, church or region. Violence, poverty or perversion may hang over your city or nation. Your children may have been taken captive by humanism or the spirit of this age. Ask the Lord to show you the stronghold, and use the weapons that He has given you to bind the strongman and take the spoils. No matter what stronghold or how large the strongman might seem, Jesus is greater. Our God is bigger.

Jesus told His disciples, "As the Father has sent Me, I also send you" (John 20:21). Deliverance from demons and tearing down strongholds are part of the believer's commission as warriors in the army of God. Being equipped and aware of our authority to disarm the demonic realm of its power and operation in our lives and the lives of others is essential to our effectiveness as storm warriors and intercessors in extending God's Kingdom in the days in which we are living.

Here is a prayer to guide you in taking authority over strongholds in your family.

Heavenly Father, I thank You for all that Jesus Christ has done for us. I thank You that the weapons of our warfare are not carnal, but they are mighty through God for the pulling down of strongholds. I thank You, Jesus, that You purchased redemption for all of mankind; therefore, You purchased redemption for my loved ones. In the name of Jesus, I take authority over the strongman over my family. I take authority specifically over the strongman of [name the specific strongman over your situation here, such as idolatry, alcoholism, racism or anger. Take authority over it in the name of Jesus.]

I take authority over the spirit of religious tradition, witch-craft, the occult, humanism, intellectualism, the spirit of the world, the spirit of blindness, the spirit of infirmity, all these powers. The Word of God says that whatever I bind on earth is bound in heaven. I bind this strongman over my family. I take authority over Satan and his principalities that rule over my family by the blood of Jesus, and I command you foul powers to let my family go in the name of Jesus! Amen.

10

Breakthrough in the Storm

So the sun stood still in the midst of heaven, and did not hasten to go down for about a whole day. And there has been no day like that, before it or after it, that the Lord heeded the voice of a man; for the Lord fought for Israel. Then Joshua returned, and all Israel with him, to the camp at Gilgal.

Joshua 10:13–15

Every battle has a turning point, the strategic moment when one of the armies gains the high ground in the struggle and the tide shifts in that force's favor.

In the long days of World War II, one of these turning points came in mid-December 1944. German soldiers had caught Allied forces by surprise and penetrated their lines of defense deep into Belgium. This dent or "bulge" in the lines began the legendary four-week standoff that became known as the Battle of the Bulge. Many accounts of heroism and bravery on the part of the American troops emerged as the smoke cleared from the battle. One story stands out as our favorite of the character that it takes to stand for breakthrough.

Late on the night of December 23, the last American troops were pulling out of the village of Provedroux. The Germans were closing in on the burning village from three sides, and soldiers, many separated from their units during the wild retreat, scrambled to catch a ride out of the village any way they could.

One such soldier found himself waved aboard a tank destroyer as an entire U.S. armored division rolled through the town. They had just reached the highway through the Ardennes forest when the lieutenant aboard spotted a lone American private digging a foxhole. Grimy from days on the battlefield and armed with only a bazooka and a rifle, the private went about his business without a glance at the long line of retreating vehicles passing by.

The lieutenant ordered his vehicle to pull up alongside the soldier. Barely pausing in his task, the private looked up and said, "If yer looking for a safe place, just pull that vehicle behind me. I'm the 82nd Airborne. This is as far as those **** are going."

The soldiers on the tank destroyer looked at one another. They were weary from the constant retreat of the previous week. But another glance at the paratrooper convinced them. The lieutenant gave the order: "You heard the man. Let's set up for business!"

Soon two truckloads of GIs joined the roadblock. Throughout the night soldiers trickled in, and their defenses grew in strength and number. Before long that one man's determination led to a major strongpoint in the battle. From that stance the Allies were able to beat back the German offensive. His refusal to retreat changed the course of the war, and, thereby, history.

This gives a picture of what Christ has done for us. Jesus dug in against the enemy lines as He prepared for the great battle on the cross. While the world was retreating in the face of sin and death, Christ volunteered to take a stand. Clothed in the ragged humility of the weakness of human flesh, armed with only the companionship of the Holy Spirit and His own willingness to lay down His life, He "set up for business."

The night before that great battle Jesus sat with His friends, presenting the bread and wine as His own body and blood. He was declaring that by offering Himself, everyone who sought a safe place from the advancing kingdom of darkness would forever be able to take a stand behind Him.

When Jesus went to the Garden to watch and pray beyond the Temple Mount, He asked three of His closest friends to watch with Him. "Tarry here while I go over there and pray," He said. He did not ask them to shoulder His burden but to stay as friends and keep watch while He entered His passion. We learn a great lesson for our generation as we remember that those friends all fell asleep because of the great anxiety of the hour. As darkness and spiritual tensions increase, it is all the more essential that we encourage one another daily and stay vital in the Holy Spirit. Jesus is seeking a few friends who will stay alert and watch with Him in this hour.

After Jesus accomplished His great victory against the powers of darkness, He left simple yet profound instructions for all who would follow Him. He commanded that we preach the Gospel throughout the world with miracles attesting to it until He returns. And He said to watch and pray until He appeared in the clouds of His coming: "What I say to you I say to all, watch and pray."

But it is in Gethsemane that we hear the disturbing question: "Could you not watch with Me one hour?" That was the hour in which Christ set up for business against the kingdom of darkness. The victory that He won on Calvary began in the darkness under the ancient olives in the Garden, trees that still pour out their oil. It is as if the Light of the world is looking down upon the earth, searching for those watchtowers where the oil lamps of the Gospel are burning brightly into the long night. Those steady flames shall light the way when He comes to gather His bride.

Building Your Breakthrough

In the days of Samuel and David we read of many significant moments in Israel's national history—turning points, defeat of enemies, encounters with God and with their destiny—all of which occur at Mizpah. The name is given to several places in ancient Israel: Mizpah of Judah, Gilead, Moab and Mount Hermon are all places of strategic personal and national importance. In Hebrew *mizpah* means "watchtower" and represents security. Mizpah is the place where people gather to recommit themselves to God and pray for His breakthrough against their enemies. Mizpah is a seat of government. It is the place you get your bearings to go from one point to the next.

Here are some of the things that occur at Mizpah. Every home should become a watchtower for these blessings.

The Lord "watches" between you and your enemies (see Genesis 31:49).

Victory over kings and armies for control of the region is given (see Joshua 11:3).

Inheritance is allotted (see Joshua 15:38).

Righteous persons are acknowledged as heads and chiefs (see Judges 11:11).

People assemble in unity "as one man" (see Judges 20:1).

Wickedness is exposed and banished (see Judges 20:3).

Covenant is made (see Judges 21).

Cleansing and deliverance take place (see 1 Samuel 7:6).

Enemies are subdued (see 1 Samuel 7:11).

Righteous judgments are made (see 1 Samuel 7:16).

Visitation and refreshing in the anointing are given (see 1 Samuel 7:16–17).

Family members are protected (see 1 Samuel 22:3).

Fortification is offered during times of conflict (see 1 Kings 15:22).

Idolatry and perversion are torn down (see 1 Kings 15:12).

Treasures are recovered (see 1 Kings 15:15).

Governors are enthroned (see Nehemiah 3:7).

Rebuilding, covering and fortification are done (see Nehemiah 3:15).

Repairs are made (see Nehemiah 3:19).

Refuge is given the righteous when violence overruns the land (see Jeremiah 40:6).

Dwelling places are given to servants of the Lord (see Jeremiah 40:6).

The remnant escapes bondage (see Jeremiah 40:11).

The hungry are fed with the best produce of the land (see Jeremiah 40:12).

It is the place of turnaround and return (see Jeremiah 41:14).

Another central location of God's Mizpah is the local church body that is moving in the anointing of the Holy Spirit. We encourage you to find and stay connected to your local spiritual family. One of the enemy's most effective tactics is separating believers from the rest of the members of Christ's Body. If you can be offended, you will be. If you are a wanderer, no church will satisfy you. If you are a rebel, no spiritual leader will be "anointed" enough or "prophetic" enough to tell you what to do. But if you stay in that state, you will eventually be cut off from your reward.

The Bible is very clear about Christians gathering within a given locale as a worshiping band of prayer warriors and living out their lives in long-term love and commitment toward one another. It is much easier to be overcome by the battle when we are facing it alone. We need each other and the strength we can gain from the Body of Christ as we take our stand as warriors together. As you build the watchtower of prayer and fasting and fortify its walls with righteousness and thanksgiving, you are providing security for your family and the community around you.

As you light the lamps of the Mizpah and welcome the Holy Spirit, the government of God can come down to settle upon your land. In His peace you and your children will find peace. From the watchtower God will give supernatural intelligence for all that concerns you. He will keep His eye on the enemies that rise up against you. He will make you a light for others who sit in darkness. And He will judge and cleanse you and make you a storm warrior of the King.

The Lord of the Breakthrough

When our lives are submitted to the Lord, tempests that would normally destroy us simply propel us to our destiny faster. The vehicle of a challenge or crisis can reveal the plan of our victorious God and give us greater momentum for reaching it. God has proven over and over that He brings breakthrough in the storm.

> David inquired of God, saying, "Shall I go up against the Philistines? Will You deliver them into my hand?" The LORD said to him, "Go up, for I will deliver them into your hand." So they went up to Baal Perazim, and David defeated them there. Then David said, "God has broken through my enemies by my hand like a breakthrough of water." Therefore they called the name of that place Baal Perazim [or Master of Breakthrough].
>
> 1 Chronicles 14:10–11

Breakthroughs are the result of a tremendous buildup of pressure. When a dam is breached, the floodwaters thunder forward, swallowing everything in their path. This is the victory described by David. God stands ready to do the same for you.

Your faith in God and the small measures of simple obedience you do every day are building to critical mass for your breakthrough. Pressure is building as you persevere through discipline and righteousness. It builds as you hold your ground and trust in what the Bible says. It builds as you endeavor to believe the impossible.

One thing is certain: God is the Master of our Breakthrough. His blessing overpowers any curse, removes any hindrance, takes down any giant that stands in His way. It is like the flood when He comes. He washes His enemies out of His path. And though He may seem long in coming, wait for Him. Continue to fast and pray. Do the little things He tells you. Even now the pressure of His blessing is building up behind the obstacle you face. As you pray and fast, the wall is cracking. Add to the pressure by thanking God and others for everything. Steadfast confidence—expressed through praise for the greatness of God in the face of our enemy—releases the overflowing power for breakthrough. Before long the wall will come crashing down.

Sometimes people give up just before their breakthrough. David sang these words to the Lord after a great deliverance: "I have pursued my enemies and overtaken them; neither did I turn back again till they were destroyed" (Psalm 18:37). God wants us to hand our enemies utter defeat. His intention is not that we settle for a cease-fire or leave the battlefield before the victory is won.

When dealing with the devil, appeasement is not an option. We often hear of governments "making painful concessions" in order to "make peace" with a sworn enemy. This only gives the enemy a stronger foothold. The enemy's old spiritual tactic is to try and wear down the righteous by drawing out pain and oppression. Christians cannot allow difficulty or pain to become the cause for compromise. We must allow the Lord to make us battle-hardened, rather than allowing the devil to make us battle-weary.

A New Perspective

God is giving a new perspective to His people. He is loosening the scales that have grown over the eyes of those He is calling to become mighty. Like entering a 3-D movie, we are experiencing the reality of spiritual conflict and conquest as never before. Spiritual matters that were once distant, flat-screened theories are suddenly larger than life all around us. The person closest to you may be unable to see through the lenses of Holy Spirit perspective that God is giving you. But with the eyes of the Spirit you are seeing things differently than you once did, and you find yourself right in the midst of the action.

Your hour has come! You may never have imagined yourself as a mighty warrior of faith and courage. Maybe you have seen yourself as nothing more than another face blending into a crowd of common people living a common life.

King David grew up as a simple shepherd boy. During those years in the fields protecting his father's flocks from lions and bears, David grew in courage and faithfulness. Those days and nights were his training ground for the spiritual and natural war that was coming upon the kingdom in his day. Because he developed a relationship of trust with the God of Israel, David became a strongpoint around which the distressed, discontent, in-debt men of Israel could rally for a turnaround in their lives and nation.

> David therefore departed from there and escaped to the cave of Adullam. So when his brothers and all his father's house heard it, they went down there to him. And everyone who was in distress, everyone who was in debt, and everyone who was discontented gathered to him. So he became captain over them. And there were about four hundred men with

169

him. Then David went from there to Mizpah [the watch-tower] of Moab.

1 Samuel 22:1–3

Distressed, in debt and discontented—a veritable 3-D army—these men would rise out of the flat routines of their lives to become heroes for God. Many of them rose to the occasion because they had been backed into a corner and had nothing more to lose. Their very existence threatened, they finally said, "Enough is enough. This is as far as those so-and-sos are going!" These men exhibited the mindset of storm warriors. Their difficulties, bitter experiences and challenging circumstances led them to take a stand. This is the response the Holy Spirit yearns for in the lives of those who know Christ intimately.

Among these followers were David's mighty men of valor. These men performed exploits while ordinary soldiers were fleeing in terror. When the storm strikes, the persons whose strength is in the Lord will rise to take a stand against His enemies. Like many apostles of our faith, their names are recorded as ones who were willing to lay down their lives for the cause.

These are the names of the mighty men whom David had: Josheb-Basshebeth the Tachmonite, chief among the captains. He was called Adino the Eznite, because he had killed eight hundred men at one time. And after him was Eleazar the son of Dodo, the Ahohite, one of the three mighty men with David when they defied the Philistines who were gathered there for battle, and the men of Israel had retreated. He arose and attacked the Philistines until his hand was weary, and his hand stuck to the sword. The LORD brought about a great victory that day; and the people returned after him only to plunder. And after him was Shammah the son of Agee the Hararite. The Philistines had gathered together into a troop where there was a piece of ground full of lentils. So the people fled from the Philistines. But he stationed himself in the middle of the field, defended it, and killed the Philistines. So the LORD brought about a great victory.

2 Samuel 23:8–12

The Tachmonite was chief of three who accompanied David. *Tachmonite* means "one who possesses insight and practical wisdom." Even the most profoundly spiritual warfare requires some practical wisdom for implementation. God gives us the Holy Spirit and godly spiritual leaders to help answer our questions and direct His battle plan. That is why people who are easily offended will have difficulty becoming storm warriors. Following the battle plan even when your leaders seem to be making tactical mistakes will position you to do exploits.

Eleazar the son of Dodo fought with such intensity that afterward his sword stuck to his hand. In this respect the sword represents the Word of God—just as Jesus used the Word to defy Satan by declaring, "It is written!" *Eleazar* means "the Lord is my helper." *Dodo* is Hebrew for "loving," and *Ahohite* is a word meaning "brotherhood." This represents a man who is able to do warfare from a standpoint of love for his brethren. Determined and loyal, his hand becomes one with the weapon of the Word. He wields the sword of the Spirit for the cause of the king.

When the medical experts told us Aaron would die, we chose to become one with the word God had given us: *You will have a son.* The supernatural glory of God gave us our breakthrough, but we refused to give up the territory of our inheritance even in the face of death. The greatest storm

171

warriors will be those who love the brethren and become one with the purposes of God to bring about His glory.

Shammah, son of Agee the Hararite, took his stand against the Philistines in a field of lentils when Israel's army fled. The lentil field represented the inheritance and future provision for the families of Israel. Shammah defended those lentils with his life and by doing so struck down giant Philistines. He risked death for a bean patch because it was a strategic position in the battle, and would be a source of perpetual provision for generations to come. The devil and his legions have been stealing pieces of our inheritance for many centuries. Part of every Christian's personal inheritance is the power of the Spirit manifest in healing, deliverance and miracles. It is time for a generation of spiritual storm warriors to take a stand for that inheritance and recover it for our children.

People who are uncomfortable with the works of our Father have made it religiously incorrect to talk of miracles, much less do them. But the Church is rising up to take back her heritage one lentil field at a time!

Shammah means "ruin or desolation"; *Agee* means "a flame." It is not unusual for the person destined to carry the fire of God to seem like a wreck at first. Sometimes our greatest losses become the fuel for the mightiest victories. As the Holy Spirit comes, the fire of God's glory is shown. The anointing that breaks the yoke is released in the power of Pentecost.

It is not by our might or according to the power we possess but by God's Spirit that we will prevail. This promise from Scripture is true for everyone who believes in Jesus. Out of his or her belly will come rushing a living flood of spiritual force to overwhelm wickedness. When Jesus said, "I will come to you," He was referring to the outpouring of His Spirit.

Take courage today by the Spirit and rise to the occasion. Let the Lord show you what to do and how to accomplish the task before you. You fight for the King and His eternal Kingdom. Such was the vision of the heroes who took their stand as David's mighty men. They did not appear to be heroes. Some of them were simply fed up with being overrun by their enemies. But they recognized the anointing on the king and chose to get in on the action. They used the bitter things in their lives as opportunities for breakthrough in their generation.

God is not afraid of a challenge. He shows Himself most glorious when He intervenes in power in our otherwise hopeless situations. The more difficult the problem you are facing the greater opportunity for God to show Himself strong in and through you!

Mighty Men Still Needed

We live in an hour in which the old specter of assault on liberty is rising again. Be it philosophically in our public education, spiritually through compromise in our Christian foundations, morally through political correctness or internationally from terrorists seeking to dominate the world, the people who know their God must arise and do exploits in the power of the Spirit and the truth of His Word.

David's mighty men were not conscripted; they were volunteers. When you show up to do whatever needs to be done simply because it is truly in your heart to serve, God can use you. It really does not matter what kind of condition you are in otherwise. These men began as a bunch of rejects. Yet they had what God was looking for: willing hearts. They loved David and honored the anointing on his life so much that they fought through enemy lines just to get him some water from the well in Bethlehem (see 2 Samuel 23:15–17). They laid down their lives because it was in their hearts to do so.

We follow in the long line of storm warriors throughout the ages who have believed there is something worth dying for. Abraham was a simple herdsman. Yet he obeyed God's voice to travel to a distant land and live among strangers. One time, confronting the armies of five kings, he took just 318 men into battle and defeated them all. He was a warrior.

Moses got his orders from the Commander in Chief: "I want you to face down the world's most powerful man and arrange the release of two million people from his nation." By God's power it happened!

Samson slew a thousand with the jawbone of a donkey. He destroyed more enemies in his death than in his life.

Daniel was unafraid to go into the lions' den. John the Baptist met death without fear. Paul braved storm after storm and was, ultimately, poured out as a drink offering.

Like the well water David poured out as an offering before God, their lives were not wasted. When we choose to make the things that are special to God special to us, God will choose to make the things that are special to us special to Him. Our priorities are most clearly seen through our prayers. If we come to God with a long list of "I want, I need, me this, me that," we must wonder if it grieves His heart. The bonds of love are tested the greatest when someone is always needing, demanding, using others for personal edification. Rather, let us look for ways to serve by making a priority of the things that matter to those we love, beginning with our love for Jesus. It pleases His heart for His ambassadors on earth to come to Him daily in their prayers, making His priorities their own.

Become What You Believe

> As Jesus left the house, he was followed by two blind men crying out, "Mercy, Son of David! Mercy on us!" When Jesus got home, the blind men went in with him. Jesus said to them, "Do you really believe I can do this?" They said, "Why, yes, Master!" He touched their eyes and said, "Become what you believe." It happened. They saw.
>
> Matthew 9:27–30, MESSAGE

Every storm warrior must see himself through the truth of what Scripture tells us about ourselves in God. Condition your mind for victory. Do not allow your past to define your future. Praise God who *always* leads us in triumph in Christ and you will find that He will turn your greatest disappointments into your greatest places of victory.

A key to your breakthrough is your willingness to battle through even in the face of death. When you do not fear for your life, the enemy has no hold over you. Sometimes that death is manifested in us by letting go of past offenses. Sometimes it is by relinquishing our insistence on having our own way. Sometimes it is by laying down a dream or vision in order to serve God more fully. Sometimes it is by being willing to sacrifice our own comfort, convenience or well-being so that others might be promoted or that God might be glorified. Sometimes it is by humbling ourselves before others and always it is by humbling ourselves before God. Jesus took every offense upon Himself on the cross. When we die to our right to hold on to them, resurrection life is released in our hearts. Instead of seeking justification, we become the righteousness of God by forgiving. We step over into the realm of liberty where the just man lives by his faith.

Joseph's life is a lesson in the power of forgiveness. He was thrown into the pit because of the sins of others. But God used that treachery by his own family to set Joseph's feet on the path to a great destiny. Joseph had plenty of reason to hold a lasting grudge of bitterness, but he did not define himself according to the sins of others or the pit they threw him into. Down in that darkness Joseph remembered the dream God had given him. He held on to the vision before him. Joseph defined himself according to the ability of God to perform His word. "They hurt his feet with fetters, he was laid in irons. Until the time that his word came to pass, the word of the LORD tested him" (Psalm 105:18–19).

Joseph's trust in the One who could deliver positioned him to be in the right place at the right time and with the right heart for the Lord to use him mightily. From his prison cell in the dungeon, Joseph was lifted up to sit beside the pharaoh of Egypt. When his moment came, all the strength of character and the power of influence he gained through his suffering became the strongpoint of breakthrough to save his entire nation in a time of crisis. In the end, the storms Joseph endured catapulted him to his destiny.

Our destiny often lies in our own decisions. Our responses determine the course of the storm and its impact on many lives. Offense, anger, bitterness, jealousy, self-pity and the like will cause us to flounder. "Keep your heart with all diligence, for out of it spring the issues of life. Put away from you a deceitful mouth, and put perverse lips far from you" (Proverbs 4:23–24).

In our years of ministry we have seen many break-throughs delayed because of heart issues. God is in the business of healing broken hearts! Repent and take your disappointments, betrayals and heartbreaks to Him. Move on into the victory He has assured us in the power of His resurrection.

> The world is unprincipled. It's dog-eat-dog out there! The world doesn't fight fair. But we don't live or fight our battles that way—never have and never will. The tools of our trade aren't for marketing or manipulation, but they are for demolishing that entire massively corrupt culture. We use our powerful God-tools for smashing warped philosophies, tearing down barriers erected against the truth of God, fitting every loose thought and emotion and impulse into the structure of life shaped by Christ. Our tools are ready at hand for clearing the ground of every obstruction and building lives of obedience into maturity.
>
> 2 Corinthians 10:3–6, MESSAGE

We have been given authority in the spiritual realm through the victory of Jesus' death and resurrection. We must lay hold of this truth personally if we are to provide breakthrough for the generation coming after us. Storms in our families may be preparing us to be storm warriors for nations. And natural circumstances, personalities, cultures, governments and society all reflect the larger spiritual battlefield that we cannot always see. Recognizing our authority in the face of these storms will help us respond with supernatural peace and grace.

No weapon formed against us, be it natural or spiritual, can withstand the power and authority of God the Holy Spirit who dwells in us. This revelation will transform the way we respond. As we gain victory in the realms closest to us, we pass the blessings on to our children and our children's children.

Finally, my brethren, be strong in the Lord and in the power of His might. . . . For we do not wrestle against flesh and blood, but against principalities, against powers, against the rulers of the darkness of this age, against spiritual hosts of wickedness in the heavenly places. Therefore take up the whole armor of God, that you may be able to withstand in the evil day, and having done all, to stand . . . being watchful to this end with all perseverance and supplication for all the saints.

Ephesians 6:10, 12–13, 18

The Greatest Spirit

I, Mahesh, will always remember a particular instance when the Holy Spirit put me in a position to become a strongpoint for breakthrough for many who lived in a region oppressed by dark sorcerers and witch doctors for many years. I was completely willing but used totally unwittingly by the Lord that day! Everyone present witnessed the resurrection power of Jesus over advancing lines of darkness.

We were holding a series of meetings in a region of the Congo that was notorious for being a center of witchcraft and sorcery. Thousands of people were being saved and delivered through our meetings. Angered by our presence and the power of the anointing, the local contingency of witch doctors hired the chief sorcerer to go to our meetings and place a curse on me. In Africa if a witch doctor tells someone he is going to die at the end of the day, he dies at the end of the day. Their power is real.

At that particular meeting there were more than five thousand people waiting for me to pray for them. The local pastors recognized the sorcerer, but they were so afraid they did not tell me he was there. The man joined the thousands of others in the healing line and waited for me to approach so he could curse me. As I went down the line, I laid hands on everyone and prayed, "Bless, bless him, Lord. Heal him. . . ."

As I came to the chief sorcerer, his eyes turned back in his head; all I could see were the whites of his eyes. He put out his hands toward me and voices that were animal, human, male, female, lion and cougar started coming out of his mouth all at once. I had clear discernment at that moment. I said, "This man has problems!" But my hair was standing on end because I knew that a major spiritual confrontation was taking place. Normal human beings do not have multiple voices coming out of them simultaneously. I laid my hand on him and said, "Jesus, bless him."

Instantly his body flew through the air over the heads of the people. He hit the dirt so hard I cringed. He was down on the ground and could not get up, writhing and turning in his struggle. Powerless to resist the Lord, the chief sorcerer roared in anger at being humiliated in the eyes of thousands of people. I watched for a few minutes and said again, "Well, Lord, bless him." Then I continued to pray for the rest of the people.

Thirty minutes later I came back to get a drink of water and this man was standing with the pastors. He started trembling as I walked toward him. He said, "I know spirits, and the Spirit over this man is greater than any spirit that I have ever seen!" The sorcerer had been unable to get up until he had confessed Jesus as Lord. That day we experienced firsthand the truth of God's power: "Greater is he that is in you, than he that is in the world" (1 John 4:4, KJV).

One man took a stand two thousand years ago; He planted a standard, and opened the double doors for deliverance, for adoption by God, for salvation, healing and eternal life for every person. We are His friends and standard bearers. He has called us to become a point of breakthrough in a life, in a family, in a community, in a nation, in a generation. You can become the strongpoint to turn the tide back to God in this hour. You are the key for the turning point. When you are born again you are endowed with the Spirit of God. The same Holy Spirit who raised Jesus from the dead and who conquered every demonic power in that former sorcerer resides in you and in me.

Jesus said, "You will receive power." Jesus has come into His Garden seeking those closest friends who are willing to join Him, a band of storm warriors of the Spirit who will watch and pray with Him. He is seeking all those who will risk their lives in their generation to make a breakthrough for God.

When you have done everything else, take a stand; hold your ground against the enemy. And expect breakthrough.

11

RULES OF ENGAGEMENT

"Behold, I give you the authority to trample on serpents and scorpions, and over all the power of the enemy, and nothing shall by any means hurt you."

Luke 10:19

I, Mahesh, often tell this story from Bonnie's days growing up on a cattle ranch in New Mexico. During one of the cattle drives, she and her cousins were playing "hide and seek" in the barn. Scarcely had she pressed herself into a dark corner among some feed barrels when she heard a dry, rattling sound—and felt something erupt at her feet. The next thing she knew, heart in her throat, she was out of the barn and in the ranch house, jumping up and down on her one remaining sandal, shouting, "Snake! Snake!"

Her father and uncles rushed to the barn. After they found and killed the snake, her father lifted it up with a shovel for her to see. There, still tightly clamped in the fangs of the three-foot rattler, was Bonnie's other sandal!

This heart-pounding episode in her life gives a good picture of how the enemy works. Like the snake lurking in that dark corner of the barn, the devil will lurk in hidden places, waiting for an opportune time to strike. If he can, he will engage us in battle under his rules and on his timetable. His strategy is to distract us from God's big picture—from our biblical priorities—and keep us on the defensive. Yet if we learn the Lord's rules of engagement, we can turn the tables on our adversary.

Bonnie remembers looking forward to the summers when the family moved the herds to higher pastures on Taylor Mountain. The climate was too cool and the elevation too high for snakes to dwell. There above the "snake line" she could play freely with no fear of an accidental encounter.

This story illustrates two important points. First, Jesus said that we shall tread upon snakes and scorpions and they will not hurt us. But, second, we need to realize that we can actually get above the "spiritual snake line" where even the most lethal predators cannot dwell.

The Bible tells us of this place that we enter with the Lord where the enemy will not even venture: "Now it shall come to pass in the latter days that the mountain of the LORD's house shall be established on the top of the mountains, and shall be exalted above the hills; and peoples shall flow to it" (Micah 4:1). Jesus took Peter, James and John up the mountain and was transfigured before them (see Matthew 17). The apostle John wrote that a voice like a trumpet called to him: "Come up here" (Revelation 4:1).

The Lord is calling His storm warriors to dwell there, above the snake line. Job 28:7–8 proclaims, "There is a path which no fowl knoweth, and which the vulture's eye hath not seen: the lion's whelps have not trodden it, nor the fierce lion passed by it" (KJV). The mountain of the Lord is higher than every other plane in heaven and earth. It is the place where we are already seated in Christ Jesus. There the air is the *Ruach Ha Kodesh*, the very breath of God. The anointing revives the spirit, breaks every yoke and causes the devil to flee.

In this chapter we will learn to take the offensive in our battle with the enemy. We will study rules of engagement that help us understand the plans and purposes that God has for us. These are tactics that keep us safe as we tread on serpents and that also take us above the snake line. How do we go up to the mountain? Let's find out.

Let Your Praises Be Heard

Have you ever watched one of those nature documentaries on giant boa constrictors? They can literally asphyxiate an animal and swallow it whole! Entire pigs, dogs—even deer!—can wind up victims of the snake's digestive tract.

Now, these powerful creatures do not start out life as fearsome monsters; they start out as tiny little snakes. In other words, they are manageable when they are small, but they grow into dangerous predators. This is why, every once in a while, you read about a person being killed by a "pet" python.

It is the same in the spirit. If we allow the enemy to gain even the smallest place in our hearts or minds, he will use it to destroy us. There are spiritual snakes that wrap themselves around our lives and families with the intent of slowly squeezing the life out of us.

The first rule of engagement for warriors in the face of the enemy might not seem strong enough in the face of such evil power, but few weapons are more successful at keeping the enemy from gaining a position of dominance.

This rule is praise—and it includes worship, thanksgiving and praying in the Spirit. David modeled this for us in the Psalms of Ascent, praises sung to God as the nation of Israel ascended the hill of the Lord. The ascent begins at a low point in Psalm 120 with the distress of a man who finds himself dwelling in the midst of treachery and violence with no means of escape. In fifteen steps, like the rungs of a ladder, he sings his way out of the pit. Ascending higher and higher, at last he stands, anointed with priestly oil, before the double doors that are the gates of the sanctuary where the manifest Presence of God rested. Those doors will open for him of their own accord, and he shall enter with thanksgiving and praise to commune with God all night in worship.

Praise will sever the head of the serpent and also take us into an atmosphere where no evil can dwell. A heart full of praise and worship at all times and in every circumstance is a weapon that we need to wield in our lives personally, in our homes, in our families, in our churches and in our nations. If the enemy cannot destroy us, he will try to keep us from climbing higher through his noxious lies and poisonous bite, but a heart that praises the Lord will not be overcome.

Praise is an end time apostolic weapon that God is restoring to His Church. You will recall the story of how, at midnight, in the darkest hour and in a dank and filthy dungeon crawling with cockroaches and rats, Paul and Silas offered up praise to God. "Suddenly there was a great earthquake, so that the foundations of the prison were shaken; and immediately all the doors were opened and everyone's chains were loosed" (Acts 16:26). The delivering power of God came in on their praise, opening *every* door in the prison. Our praise affects more than just our personal circumstances. Just as it loosed the chains of those who were captive with Paul and Silas, so praise has the power to loose the chains of injustice in the world around us and set prisoners free.

During one of our watch services a wave of glory swept over the congregation, and we entered a realm of praise that is hard to describe in human language. We were on the mountain of the Lord. Out of His glorious presence I felt the Lord say, *This is one of the primary ways that I am going to give My people victory over whatever the enemy has waged against them.*

We live in a season in which the darkness is getting darker. Pythons that used to be small and merely a nuisance have wrapped themselves around entire nations. In America, secular humanists would like us to believe that our godly foundations have been squeezed out of existence. Terrorism threatens to asphyxiate whole regions, with the ultimate goal of destroying Israel. Yet through praise we wield a spiritual weapon that can deliver us from the suffocating power of these demonic forces.

As we studied earlier, Acts 28 recounts Paul's miraculous escape from a shipwreck. Almost immediately after setting foot on solid ground he was bitten on the hand by a deadly snake. The inhabitants of the island took this to be a sign that this particular prisoner surely deserved judgment, but Paul simply shook off the snake without any ill effects.

Because Paul had cultivated a lifestyle of praise and thanksgiving, he was able to live with sure and steady confidence in God's power to save him. Imprisonment, shipwrecks and venomous snakes would dot Paul's journey, but his destination was sure. Nothing could stand in the way of his mission to proclaim the Word of God.

As warriors we will find that praise helps us continue unwavering in our faith as well. We will not let the enemy have even the smallest point of entry, knowing that it could grow into a stranglehold on our lives. Cultivating a lifestyle of praise, worship and praying in the Spirit is our key to staying focused on our mission. It takes us to the lofty places on the mountain.

Prepare for Battle

Our next rule of engagement comes from Paul's letter to the Ephesians, in which the apostle likened the Church to an army preparing for battle. It was an illustration that his readers would have understood instantly. The Roman army was the most formidable force of its time. Its widespread presence enforced the far reaches of the Roman Empire. Paul was intimately acquainted with the soldier's life, spending the last years of his life under guard. He respected the soldier's discipline, training and dedication. When he described himself as bearing in his body "the marks of the Lord Jesus" (Galatians 6:17), he was referring to a brand on the back of the left hand that a Roman soldier received as a mark of honor upon completing basic training.

Paul used the familiar terminology of the superpower of his day to instruct and encourage the Church to stand victorious in every storm. We have looked at parts of this passage of Scripture that follows. Here is a fuller context:

> Finally, my brethren, be strong in the Lord and in the power of His might. Put on the whole armor of God, that you may

be able to stand against the wiles of the devil. For we do not wrestle against flesh and blood, but against principalities, against powers, against the rulers of the darkness of this age, against spiritual hosts of wickedness in the heavenly places. Therefore take up the whole armor of God, that you may be able to withstand in the evil day, and having done all, to stand. Stand therefore, having girded your waist with truth, having put on the breastplate of righteousness, and having shod your feet with the preparation of the gospel of peace; above all, taking the shield of faith with which you will be able to quench all the fiery darts of the wicked one. And take the helmet of salvation, and the sword of the Spirit, which is the word of God; praying always with all prayer and supplication in the Spirit, being watchful to this end with all perseverance and supplication for all the saints.

Ephesians 6:10–18

These are the instructions of a seasoned warrior to his troops to prepare and protect them in the coming battles. All soldiers drill for battle on a regular basis; their lives depend on their ability to react under fire and use their equipment with quickness and precision. Paul taught his readers to do the same.

His first command is to "be strong." This is the Greek word *endunamoo*, which refers to the strength and courage that is received from the *dunamis* power of the Holy Spirit. A storm warrior places his confidence in the Lord and His power. This is a military stance not unlike training in martial arts. When your feet are planted solidly, your adversary cannot throw you off balance or knock you down.

Paul's next command is to take up the armor of God. As with any soldier, daily training with our equipment is essential for the day of battle. As pastors, Bonnie and I have found that one of the biggest mistakes leaders can make is to send eager and willing soldiers into battle before they have been trained and discipled. It is easy to feel ready for the big fights after an exciting meeting, but zeal alone will not win a war!

Paul's final command is to pray in the Spirit and watch in prayer. Cultivating a relationship with the Holy Spirit and watching and praying corporately are all disciplines of an effective spiritual army. Storm warriors learn to be sensitive to the Holy Spirit through their foundation in the Word of God and their relationships with other men and women who are disciples. There are no lone rangers, and there are no armies of one. Soldiers who are prepared for battle are those who are joined to a company. They are loyal, faithful and under command.

The Lord uses the local body and the leaders in our lives to train us up into maturity and readiness for every battle. Defining your mission and commission in the context of your local spiritual family is one of the foundational principles in finding your identity and destiny in the army of God.

Learn from Ancient Principles

In the year 400 B.C., the vast landscape of China was ruled by any number of kings and feudal lords. Their survival was contingent upon their armies' ability to defend and expand their territories. One of these kings, King Ho Lu, was presented with thirteen chapters of soldiering theory by an unknown native of his state named Sun Tzu. The manuscript, called *The Art of War*, made intriguing reading. The king summoned Sun Tzu to court. This story, adapted from Sun

Tzu, *The Art of War* (edited by James Clavell, New York: Delacorte Press, 1983), tells what happened.

The king addressed the author: "May I submit your theory to a test?"

"You may, sire," Sun Tzu replied.

"May the test be applied to women, as well as to soldiers?"

"It may," was the answer.

As the king took his place to observe the drill, 180 young ladies from the palace entourage were brought into the courtyard. Sun Tzu divided the women into two companies, placing the king's favorites as heads of each of the two divisions, and gave them these instructions: "When I say 'eyes front' you must look straight ahead. When I say 'left turn' you must face toward your right hand. When I say 'about turn' you must face right around toward the back. Do you understand?"

The girls nodded uncertainly. As drums beat a cadence, Sun Tzu commanded.

"Right turn!"

The women began giggling and turning in every direction. Sun Tzu faced the king and explained, "If words of command are not clear and distinct, the general is to blame."

Sun Tzu proceeded to drill the women again, giving them specific directions. Then he gave them a new order: "Left turn!" Again, however, amid much laughter, the young women turned in every direction.

Sun Tzu again addressed the king: "If words of command are not clear and distinct, the general is to blame. But if his orders are clear and the soldiers disobey, then it is the fault of their officers." He then ordered that the women designated as leaders of each company be beheaded. He then moved the next ones in line into their positions.

This time when he gave orders, the women modeled them flawlessly.

His experiment over, Sun Tzu turned to the king and said, "Your troops, sire, are now ready for inspection. Bid them go through fire or water and they will not now disobey."

Sun Tzu was installed as general of King Ho Lu's army. Under his leadership the army was victorious in every battle it fought.

As storm warriors we can be sure that our Commander Jesus gives His soldiers clear commands! Spiritual leaders at every level must also learn to receive and give commands that are clear and simple to obey.

We want to continue here for a few moments using some of the principles that Sun Tzu taught as illustrations for waging good warfare in the Spirit as we confront and pull down strongholds in the kingdom of darkness. *The Art of War* outlines five principles every soldier must understand, and promises that "he who knows them will not fail." They are:

The Moral Law
Heaven
Earth
The Commander
Method and Discipline

For Sun Tzu the *moral law* was the foundation for victory. The *moral law* speaks of an army's ability to have absolute confidence in the character of its commander. An army established this high ground before the fighting began so that the men in rank could obey any command coming down without hesitation, even when it put their lives on the line.

Our complete agreement with the will of God is not just our reasonable service; it is vital to our victory in battle. Jesus' triumph on the cross was possible only because He laid down His will for the will of His Father. Agonizing as He looked into the depths of God's wrath toward sin and death, Jesus prayed, "My Father, if it is possible, let this cup pass from Me; nevertheless, not as I will, but as You will." A victorious soldier is one who has a heart committed to the mission and the courage to carry it out.

Heaven signifies times and seasons. Scripture describes the sons of Issachar as those who understood the times and knew what to do (see 1 Chronicles 12:32). Daniel "understood by the books the number of the years specified by the word of the LORD through Jeremiah the prophet" (Daniel 9:2) and went into action with prayer, repentance and fasting. Storm warriors attune their hearts to discern the seasons of the Lord and carry the burden of action in response to His Word.

The term *earth* speaks of the practical elements of a battle: the physical distances, the layout of the land, the odds and risks of any given situation. The storm warrior's life is a balanced life. Faithfulness in the practical areas of our "earthly" life is just as important as our "heavenly" activities. Jewish oral tradition states: "All Torah without work will ultimately result in desolation" (chapter 2, Mishna 2). An effective storm warrior sees that both the spiritual and the natural parts of his or her life are disciplined, in order and in balance.

The Commander stands for the virtues of wisdom, sincerity, benevolence and self-discipline. There is need for a new generation of spiritual leaders whose own lives have been mentored by godly elders and who have been trained in the apostolic traits of humility, obedience and perseverance. In 2 Kings 3:11 we find this principle when, in a military crisis, King Jehoshaphat inquires if there is a prophet among the people. The reply is indicative of God's design: "Elisha the son of Shaphat is here, who poured water on the hands of Elijah." Elisha is identified as a prophet not by his gift, but by his relationship and service to Elijah. The biblical characteristics of true apostolic faith include an ongoing family relationship with the local church congregation and the anointing to move in signs and wonders.

Method and discipline is the marshalling of the army in its proper subdivisions. This includes keeping rank among the officers, the maintenance of supply roads and even the control of military expenditure. In the Body of Christ, we are trained through the discipline of serving under spiritual authority. We are accountable to this authority to fulfill our role in maintaining a battle-ready unit at all times. A mighty warrior's character is developed over time through consistent obedience and faithfulness in small things.

These five commands are a clear, simple and practical rule of engagement. They comprise the code of conduct of every storm warrior who will advance the Kingdom of heaven in victory and power.

Follow Your Commander

As I mentioned, our Captain gives us clear commands. Following His voice is the next rule for those who want to dwell on His mountain. Jesus was a not a cryptic preacher, speaking mystical words that only a few philosophers can understand. The deepest things of God are simple enough for the littlest child to grasp. His commands are clear and practical, daily drills that, if followed, will transform us into soldiers willing to brave fire and water to obey. We are not just biding our time in anticipation of some celestial battle in the future or cataclysmic clash with the forces of evil. Our daily lives are involved in something supernatural that is an advance against an opposing kingdom.

Jesus made it clear where our allegiance should lie. He said that anyone who loves his father or mother more than Him was not worthy of Him. Paul echoed this exhortation by reminding us that no good soldier entangles himself with the affairs of this life. Storm warriors have a deep foundation of personal faith in and commitment to Jesus Christ, His Kingdom and the will of the Father in his or her generation. When the storms come, only the houses built upon rock will stand.

Jesus also exhorted us to love one another "as I have loved you." His example of self-sacrificing love is the essential nature of covenant relationship with others. The fruit of our love for God is expressed through our daily life as we live out 1 Corinthians 13 in patient, consistent, long-term association.

A lone branch cannot produce a harvest. God promises to cause us to take root in order to "fill the face of the world with fruit" (Isaiah 27:6). Every storm warrior belongs in a family where he or she learns to love, serve, adapt and conquer. Loving commitment, loyalty and faithfulness to the body in which God has planted us is essential to bearing His fruit.

It is as we express this love for one another that the Great Commission—the mission of every Christian—is accomplished: to go preach the Gospel, with confirming signs and wonders, to the ends of the earth. Our "going" will be a corporate activity. We are many members of one Body and each of us has a role to play—helping, administration, miracles, healing and so on. No job is unimportant: Somebody has to hold the horses and keep the cookfire going! In 1 Samuel 30:24–25, David set a law for Israel that holds true for us today: Those who go down into battle will receive the same share as those who stay by the supplies in the back lines. Every part is important and valued. God rewards faithfulness, not position.

Make Disciples

As Brother Derek Prince often said, "There are three kinds of Christians: sheep, goats and disciples." Sheep follow their leaders willingly, looking to the shepherd for guidance, and so receive good nourishment, safety and care under a loving, watchful eye. But they do not necessarily ever grow beyond being focused on their own needs.

Goats always have a mind of their own—"but this" and "but that," disregarding their commanders' orders in favor of their own opinions or "higher revelations." They often stir up trouble and division and sometimes lead the naïve or rebellious astray.

Then there are disciples. Disciples are those who have come under the shepherd's rod to learn, to grow and to build their Father's house. Jesus was faithful as a Son in His house (see Hebrews 3:6). Likewise, disciples are faithful stewards of their Father's inheritance, in harmony with the vision and purpose of their leaders and the One who has called them. They are true sons into whose hands an inheritance can be safely entrusted.

Our next rule of engagement is to be and to make disciples.

The mobilized Church is completing the mission given us by going forward on two legs, both moving in harmony under direction from the Head. One leg is outward-looking: international outreach and apostolic teams. The other is focused at home: firmly planted local church congregations built on solid biblical foundations in the Word and enjoying healthy, stable, loving relationships. These two qualities complement and complete, stabilize and energize one another. Neither drains the other's resources, but fuels the fulfillment of the Great Commission. Without both fully functioning in healthy harmony, the Body of Christ will be hopping about unsteadily on one leg or the other!

As Jesus' disciples, we do His works. And to help us accomplish this, God has sent the Holy Spirit. Calvary laid the groundwork that Pentecost might be possible. The coming of the Holy Spirit is the seal of our inheritance of the Gospel. This is not an inheritance laid up for the future; it is to be handled, cherished, invested and spread abroad in our lifetimes. Jesus commissioned each of us to preach the Gospel with signs and wonders following (see Mark 16:15–18). Healing, deliverance and the demonstration of His power are all part of the storm warrior's climb up the mountain of God.

Know Your Enemy

"If you know the enemy and know yourself, you need not fear the results of a hundred battles. If you know yourself but not the enemy, for every victory gained you will also suffer a defeat. If you know neither the enemy nor yourself, you will succumb in every battle." This is perhaps one of the most quoted principles in *The Art of War*. Sun Tzu emphasized the importance of knowing the enemy on the field of battle.

We, too, must know about the enemy of our souls. This is our next rule of engagement.

Scripture tells us that after testing Jesus in the wilderness, Satan "departed from Him until an opportune time" (Luke 4:13). Satan is a legalist. One of his principal tactics is to magnify the small issues in order to disrupt our main mission. Emphasizing our weaknesses and harassing us for past failures are typical strategies to bring us to a standstill in our journey up the mountain. But, storm warrior, remember this: Satan roams around *like* a roaring lion. His roar may be ominous, but his teeth and claws were removed at Calvary. The devil is just a fallen angel. Jesus is the King of kings! The Lamb has triumphed over the roaring lion and set us free from the law of sin and death. The devil does not have any new strategies, only fresh opportunities. There are some simple things to know that can guard us from becoming his prey on our way up the mountainside.

The Devil Is Defeated

The devil and his angels have been defeated and stripped of their powers. Recall Colossians 2:15: "Having disarmed principalities and powers, [Jesus] made a public spectacle of them, triumphing over them in [the cross]." We read elsewhere in Scripture:

> "And they overcame him by the blood of the Lamb and by the word of their testimony, and they did not love their lives to the death. Therefore rejoice, O heavens, and you who dwell in them! Woe to the inhabitants of the earth and the sea! For the devil has come down to you, having great wrath, because he knows that he has a short time."
>
> Revelation 12:11–12

The salvation and power of Christ and His Kingdom have come. Satan may be assaulting the inhabitants of the earth in his wrath, but we have been given the keys to victory in every battle: the blood of Christ, the prophetic word of proclamation of our faith and the sacrificial willingness to spend all to gain Christ Jesus. The one who walks in this reality day by day has nothing to fear, and he possesses *certainty*, which produces in him courage and joy for daily living. The devil's time is limited and will come to a sure and utter end with the sons of God having triumphed in Christ. There are times and seasons, regions and circumstances in which the saints of God face the blunt blows of Satan's wrath. In those times and situations it is crucial that we know the enemy and his tactics.

The Devil Is a Deceiver

Everything about the devil involves falsehood, deception and opposition to the truth. Again, remember: Satan goes around *like* a roaring lion. Satan is the great pretender, a grand illusionist. His desire is to consume you in darkness, defeat and despair.

The sword of truth in Ephesians 6 is a powerful weapon. This is the double-edged sword proceeding from the mouth of Jesus. It is the Word of God that triumphs over every other word, including the lies that Satan utters. His lies and illusions are dispelled by the light of the Word. Jesus Himself is the Word, and He dwells in us through the Holy Spirit. Confident knowledge of the Word, personal and written, allows you to call the devil's bluff and to stay out of the snare of his redundant tactics. If you have fallen prey to his act, you can be free today. "You shall know the truth, and the truth shall make you free" (John 8:32).

The Devil Is the Accuser

The devil has been stripped of everything except his insider's knowledge of the human heart. His hatred for God and God's elect drives him to exploit his last competitive edge. The name *Satan* is the Greek word *katagoros*, which means "against one in the assembly" or "accuser." We believers are the favorite objects of his accusations. Accusations create division, and a divided house or a divided mind cannot prevail in times of war or peace.

We must not allow our mouths to become his instruments for accusation against ourselves or others. An effective storm warrior learns to discipline his tongue and keep himself clear of the snare of gossip, division, slander and lying. If you become the victim of false accusation, the Holy Spirit is your defense attorney, and your heavenly Father who loves you is the Judge! "'No weapon forged against you will prevail, and you will refute every *tongue* that accuses you. This is the heritage of the servants of the LORD, and this is their vindication from me,' declares the LORD" (Isaiah 54:17, NIV, emphasis added).

The Devil Depends on Our Cooperation

The devil primarily uses people. If we could measure the frequency that our spiritual battles involve our interaction with others, it would probably astound us. From personal to national levels, the devil uses people! The Bible urges us to *resist* the devil and promises that then he will flee (see James 4:7).

Jesus told His disciples to be on their guard, vigilant for the day of His return. The victorious warrior will both anticipate his Lord's return and catch the thief red-handed. Armed with faith, truth, the power of the blood and the patient endurance to watch, no storm warrior can be overcome.

Know Yourself

"[Know] this, that our old man was *crucified* with Him, that the body of sin might be done away with, that we should no longer be slaves of sin" (Romans 6:6, emphasis added).

There is a familiar saying: "A man is his own worst enemy." This is true when engaging in the clash of spiritual kingdoms. A man who is ignorant of his own tendencies to serve the desire of his flesh will succumb in every battle. Every human is born into this world bearing the sin-seeds of our fallen parents, Adam and Eve. The Good News is that the promised Seed of the woman, Christ, has crushed the power and authority of the serpent and enemy of our souls.

We were crucified with Christ "that the body of sin might be done away with." The King James word for *crucifixion* in the context of our flesh is *mortification*. While there is "no condemnation to those who are in Christ Jesus" (Romans 8:1), the rest of the verse tells us to whom this applies: those "who do not walk according to the flesh, but according to the Spirit." Knowing ourselves means giving the Spirit free reign to speak into our hearts in order to flush out the attitudes, motives and lusts of our flesh. It is an important rule of engagement. The Holy Spirit convicts us regarding our old nature. He empowers us for repentance and transforms us into the image of Christ Jesus. Correction does not mean rejection. Every legitimate son or daughter of God will have his or her character and behavior examined and adjusted from time to time by the Lord and by His servants who oversee His Church.

Do not lose heart in the battle. Even Jesus, while preparing Himself to face the ultimate storm on the cross, subjected His human nature to testing in order to make sure it was brought under discipline and complete obedience to God. This is the only path to certain success for the child of God. Jesus learned obedience through His sufferings (see Hebrews 5:8). The implication is that experience molds the soul. Like clay under the hand of the Potter, we have been dashed upon His wheel in the process of living life. It may be a dizzying, chaotic process from time to time, but He is forming vessels for His use here and now that will be worthy to adorn His house for eternity.

After being tested, Jesus came out of the wilderness in the power and victory of the Spirit. There was an increased release of the anointing. His ministry of miracles began immediately. In the Kingdom of God, "if you live it you can give it." Your testimony of victory in your own personal trials is part of your arsenal. You can impart victory to others in the places where you have been tested and prevailed. Your greatest battle can be your place of greatest triumph over the enemy.

Let the Big Define the Small

Often in the course of our ministry and travels, we are consulted by believers who are searching sincerely for their destinies—their way up the mountain of God. The contemporary culture of the charismatic church has placed such an emphasis on individual gifting and prophecy that many people have gotten lost in the details of their own personal journeys. Our advice to them is always the same: Let the big things define the small.

Without a viable frame of reference, it is impossible to chart a course to a given destination. Every child of God has a personal calling and destiny to climb higher, but navigating our way with only ourselves as a reference point is an easy way to get lost and confused. One thing is certain for every believer: We have a wonderful heavenly Father, a victorious Savior and the power of God dwelling in us through the Holy Spirit. Our Commander has commissioned us to proclaim the Gospel with signs and wonders following. This is the destination and calling of every believer; this is our reference point in our spiritual journey. Storms and setbacks are inevitable, but if we see the big picture and have it in our hearts, the small things will start taking care of themselves. Without this perspective small issues and minor details will cause us many detours and delays. Eternity and community are essential factors of every Christian's daily compass as we allow the big things to define the small.

I, Mahesh, remember an evangelistic outreach we held in a church in Brazil. A prominent woman in the community came to our meetings. She had been incapacitated by severe back pain for several years, barely able to move and incapable of even the most basic tasks to care for her husband and young daughter.

I had a word of knowledge that the Lord was touching her back. She was healed instantly! At our church service the next day, her pastor called her forward with her husband to testify of the mighty act. Because she was formerly a premier dancer, the pastor invited the couple to dance as testimony to her complete restoration. It was an incredible sight to see them move with such grace and ease. Their daughter cried with joy to see her mother finally free from pain.

The next day, however, I was shocked to learn that some religious leaders were offended that a couple had danced in church! Focusing on the small issues without the big picture will lead us astray. Jesus called the Pharisees who were enraged that He healed on the Sabbath "blind guides, who strain out a gnat and swallow a camel!" (Matthew 23:24).

Small things happen every day: We may not get the promotion we anticipated; the pastor does not greet us after church; a close friend forgets a milestone birthday; we lose our tempers at our children. How many times have we gotten sideswiped by these events? Repent, receive forgiveness and then move on. Never let the devil torment you with the details. Let the greatness of God and the mission He has granted to each of us in His Kingdom define your life and vision.

You are a storm warrior. God has destined you to follow the rules of engagement—and come up higher.

12

THE ULTIMATE
STORM WARRIOR

And when they had come to the place called Calvary, there they crucified Him.

Luke 23:33

The ultimate Storm Warrior is Jesus Christ our Lord. He fought the greatest battle in history at the cross of Calvary—a battle that He won, shocking the natural world and turning the spirit world on its ear.

In Jesus' day the cross signified the worst of rejection, humiliation and suffering. In the battle against sin and death, the mystery of God is hidden in the truth that the way up is down. The foundation of the kingdom of darkness is pride and self-serving. The Kingdom of light advances in violent opposition through humility and self-sacrifice. As the ultimate Storm Warrior, Christ reveals this unstoppable aspect of

God's nature through His death: That which is sown in death is raised in life. This flies in the face of human wisdom.

> But Jesus answered them, saying, "The hour has come that the Son of Man should be glorified. Most assuredly, I say to you, unless a grain of wheat falls into the ground and dies, it remains alone; but if it dies, it produces much grain. He who loves his life will lose it, and he who hates his life in this world will keep it for eternal life. If anyone serves Me, let him follow Me; and where I am, there My servant will be also. If anyone serves Me, him My Father will honor."
>
> John 12:23–26

In these few words the Lamb of God revealed His worldview. His flesh was repulsed by the thought of suffering and death, just as any man's would be. But the nature of God in Him could not but embrace this destiny. When is God glorified in death? When the seed that dies produces a whole harvest of human redemption. Not everyone hears the message clearly, but those who do hear it are called upon to answer.

In Jesus' death the kingdom of darkness was upended and its prisoners set free from eternal damnation. The horizontal beam bore the outstretched arms of the Savior carrying the weight of sin of this world; it was mounted upon a vertical tree reaching up toward heaven. As His whole body hung between heaven and earth, Jesus poured out His life and won the victory.

Early Christians rejoiced in this view of their Savior. They understood that the atonement provided at the cross was utter victory over sin, death and the devil. Beyond reconciliation to the Father, beyond inspiration for personal transformation, the atonement as *victory* was the dominant view held by the early Church.

Why did Christ die? To fulfill the Scripture written of Him. The prophet Isaiah, for one, points to this fulfillment in chapter 53 describing the "Suffering Servant": "He was numbered with the transgressors" (verse 12), that is, treated like a common criminal. "He was bruised for our iniquities; the chastisement for our peace was upon Him" (verse 5). But "He shall see the labor of His soul, and be satisfied" (verse 11). God promised to "divide Him a portion with the great . . . because He poured out His soul unto death. . . . He bore the sin of many, and made intercession for the transgressors" (verse 12).

One of King David's psalms offers a remarkable observation: "You have magnified Your word above all Your name" (Psalm 138:2). There was no reputation among men that Christ sought to wear as a badge affirming who He was. Instead, He sought to be nothing more than a bearer of the emblem of the eternal Word of God, spoken in order to reconcile the world to Himself. Jesus' life was His message. His example was not unlike the old "sandwich board" carriers who, for a few pennies an hour, would walk up and down the marketplace with their messages. The signboard mostly covered the fact that a man was inside.

Jesus died to fulfill His personal mission and destiny. "For this reason I have come into the world," He told His followers, "to be made a ransom for many." Even from Jesus' birth the cross cast its shadow ahead of Him. At the Babe's dedication in the Temple, Simeon and Anna both prophesied of His future glory. In the midst of that praise, however, Simeon revealed to Mary the painful days of destiny ahead: "Yes, a sword will pierce through your own soul also" (Luke 2:35). Jesus' death was central to His mission. The mystery was the manner in which Israel's Messiah would conquer despair, vanquish darkness and establish the Kingdom of God. The Victor, the conquering King of Israel, would come as a Servant and be killed rather than kill in order to set up His throne of perfect justice.

In the days after Christ's triumphant resurrection, followers of the cross considered death as nothing more than temporarily falling asleep—an action by which one was made "present with the Lord" (2 Corinthians 5:8). Any fear of suffering and death was weighed against the *chabod*, the weighty glory of God earned through obedience. This was the key to their triumph and the spiritual *shofar* to which they rallied in the face of difficulty, persecution and trouble.

It is in this willing self-sacrifice for the greater good that Christians follow their Master and become, like Him, ultimate storm warriors in this present darkness. Those of us who have come after Christ's ascension have help in our goal of being good soldiers of the cross because we have been offered the fullness of the Spirit. Our citizenship is in heaven! We do not obey the same principles as those who simply live according to the dictates of the mortal body.

Looking to the One who was lifted up on a tree we remember the strains of Isaac Watts's beautiful hymn:

> When I survey the wondrous cross
> On which the Prince of glory died,
> My richest gain I count but loss,
> And pour contempt on all my pride.
>
> Forbid it, Lord, that I should boast
> Save in the death of Christ, my Lord;
> All the vain things that charm me most,
> I sacrifice them to His blood.

See, from His head, His hands, His feet,
Sorrow and love flow mingled down;
Did e'er such love and sorrow meet,
Or thorns compose so rich a crown?

Were the whole realm of nature mine,
That were a present far too small;
Love so amazing, so divine,
Demands my soul, my life, my all.

"My Hour Has Come"

Seven times in the gospels Jesus speaks of His passion and crucifixion as "the hour" in which His mission would culminate in success. The emphasis on His death as His greatest stroke of victory over the forces of this world and the world to come helps us to realize that the cross of Jesus has nothing less than cosmic impact on every realm of our existence. Are you in despair? Look to the cross. Are you rejoicing? Look to the cross. Are you persecuted? Look to the cross. Are you favored? Look to the cross. Are you temporary? Look to the cross. Are you eternal? Look to the cross.

The spectacle of Golgotha stands center stage for angels, demons, principalities and powers through the ages.

> But you have come to Mount Zion and to the city of the living God, the heavenly Jerusalem, to an innumerable company of angels, to the general assembly and church of the firstborn who are registered in heaven, to God the Judge of all, to the spirits of just men made perfect, to Jesus the Mediator of the new covenant, and to the blood of sprinkling that speaks better things than that of Abel.
>
> Hebrews 12:22–24

How could the Creator and Giver of Life possibly be glorified through death? Jesus prayed, "I have finished the work which You have given Me to do" (John 17:4). Throughout His ministry we see Jesus doing only what He saw the Father doing—miracles of healing and deliverance confirming the Good News that the Kingdom had come. The turning point in that battle was His utter brokenness on the tree. In that work, the death of one Man, the Father was pleased. God's love was magnified and enabled. Through death that leads to life, God has been made glorious.

All of us on this earth will face our own "hour" of trial. It might be an hour that intercepts our private lives. It might be an hour that sweeps us up into the greater challenges of global history. In every case the call of God presses us into the will of the Father. As Christ offered Himself up by the Spirit, so we lend ourselves fully in mind and body to such as pleases the Father, helping accomplish His will and good pleasure at that time. Thus we enter into the glory of Christ. In a mystery we "fill up the sufferings of Christ" by entering into fellowship with Him through our death to self. As we emerge to embrace the power and victory of His resurrection, we fulfill our destinies as sons and daughters of God because "greater love has no one than this, than to lay down his life" for his Friend.

Seven Declarations of Love

This emphasis on victory through love is one that calls to the very depths of the human spirit. True love hopes for the best at all times, bears no ill toward any, believes in the impossible for good. A nineteenth-century quote from Octavius Winslow expresses it well: "Who delivered up Jesus to die? Not Judas, for money; not Pilate, for fear; not the Jews, for envy—but the Father for love!"

The inscription written and nailed over Jesus' head read: "This is the king of the Jews." This was humiliation for the Jews, as well as a warning to any contemplating insurrection against the Roman occupation under Caesar. It was also an indictment against those who crucified Him; they had put their hand against the King of heaven. It was written in three languages: Hebrew, used by the Jews, and Greek and Latin, used by the Gentiles. In a few words the entire world, Jew and Gentile, became guilty of crucifying the innocent Man.

As Jesus was lifted up in nakedness for all the world to gaze upon, He covered once and for all man's shame revealed in the Garden of Eden. He then spoke seven "words" from the cross, open expressions of His love and absolution.

"Father, Forgive Them"

"Then Jesus said, 'Father, forgive them, for they do not know what they do'" (Luke 23:34). *This word of love was unexpected and undeserved.*

It revealed the purpose for which He would hang there for the next six hours until His death—that in spite of our ignorance, we might be forgiven the sins committed against the Father who created us. It also showed that the relationship of Father and Son was fully intact in spite of His suffering.

Included in His intercession were prayers for Roman soldiers who were following orders, for Jewish authorities who viewed Him as a threat and for Pontius Pilate who had the authority to release or kill Him. He forgave those who inflicted violence upon Him, and those who jeopardized their own eternal destiny by their ignorance. In His words we see the arms of God open wide to receive the righteous and the unrighteous. All—Jew and Gentile, religious and secular—were taken into the embrace of the cross to be made one new man in Him.

While He prayed for the sinners of the world, the religious rulers mocked Him. The soldiers, also mocking, took His garments, His only possessions, and divided them among themselves. The crowd looked on in silence.

"Today You Shall Be with Me in Paradise"

"And Jesus said to him, 'Assuredly, I say to you, today you will be with Me in Paradise'" (Luke 23:43). *This word of love gives the promise of eternal life.*

One criminal beside Him, though thoroughly deserving his own judgment, asked to be delivered. He said, "Lord, remember me when You come into Your kingdom." A dying man saw the crucified Christ beside him and chose to walk through the door of salvation. When he had no other options, he looked beyond the cross to the crown and coming glory. He embraced the mercy of God. To him Jesus said, "It won't be some day far away: Before the sun sets today I will have you with Me where I am in bliss." This word gives assurance to everyone who stands on the threshold between this life and the next. He is there—both Doorkeeper and King—offering the only release from all that binds and all that burdens.

"Woman, Behold Your Son!"

Now there stood by the cross of Jesus His mother, and His mother's sister, Mary the wife of Clopas, and Mary

Magdalene. When Jesus therefore saw His mother, and the disciple whom He loved standing by, He said to His mother, "Woman, behold your son!" Then He said to the disciple, "Behold your mother!" And from that hour that disciple took her to his own home.

John 19:25–27

This word of love brings comfort and healing.

Addressing first the one who sang Him to sleep and kissed His bruised knees when He was learning to walk, and then the one who loved Him most as He sat at the table for the last time with His friends, Jesus was the supreme example of a "heart at leisure from itself, to soothe and sympathize."

Though suffering severe physical pain and enduring far more awful agony of soul, Jesus looked out through blood-blurred vision and saw her standing there, in horror at the sight of Him. Now the words of Simeon on the day of His dedication came to pass. As the sword pierced Mary's heart, her Son reached down from the cross to comfort and secure her in the arms of a faithful guardian. In the midst of personal suffering, He took care of the one who had taken care of Him. We see in His example one who never turned inward to His own grief, but remained careful even in death that provision be made for others. And from that hour the apostle John took her into his home. The true test of our love for Christ is found in the experience of those around us when we are in pain ourselves.

These first three words were spoken during the bright morning hours before noon. Heat and thirst began to compound His suffering, as not only the weight of His own body but the weight of the world hung on the nails that pierced His hands and feet. Then He entered into long, silent agony.

The first Adam was put into a deep sleep in order to bring a helpmate from his side. But this last Adam (see 1 Corinthians 15:45) would be anesthetized only when His agony was ended in the sleep of death. And out of the bloody side of the spotless Lamb would come a Church—a Bride adorned for her Husband.

"Why Have You Forsaken Me?"

"Now from the sixth hour until the ninth hour there was darkness over all the land. And about the ninth hour Jesus cried out with a loud voice, saying, . . . 'My God, My God, why have You forsaken Me?'" (Matthew 27:45–46; see also Psalm 22:1). *This word of love answers the cry of every aching heart.*

As the mysterious, supernatural three hours of darkness were lifting, Jesus spoke words that have puzzled theologians for centuries. It is likely that they express either the feeling of being abandoned by God, even when we know He has not left us alone, or else they give evidence of the doctrine of substitution wherein Christ identifies Himself with sinful man and endures separation from God that is due sinners. This has been called Jesus' "cry of dereliction." It shows that we cannot always dissect the cosmic events of the cross.

If this word reveals Jesus' frailty of flesh and lost awareness of the Father because of His agony, it is the voice of a man feeling abandoned. It is your voice when you last cried out, "Where are You, God?" in your trials.

If, on the other hand, it is the epiphany of separation from God by sin, it is the cry that satisfies every injustice ever done to an innocent man. Suspended in the heart that is fully God and fully man, it is the deepest cry of anguish of all time.

While theologians debate the depths of this word, Jesus' cry posits itself as an answer to every "why" we might ask of God. In discussing this with one of our friends recently, he reminded us that the deepest things of God are simple enough for a child to grasp. Then he said, "I thought of Jesus' cry and immediately heard the many times I have said the same thing to God in the midst of a trial."

Once when we were in the depth of our trial over Aaron's life, Mahesh was answering the Lord's direction to be in Africa and I, Bonnie, was keeping vigil through long nights. On a certain rainy, gray afternoon as Aaron was in yet another operation to repair his gut, which had been gangrenous at his birth, I stood under the hospital portico and asked, "Why?" I will never forget the answer that came, soft and certain: *I am here with you, and that is more than enough.* The answer to every "why" that comes to our lips in times of trial, suffering or challenge is the Presence of the One who loved us and gave Himself for us.

When our human suffering leads us to question why, we can remember that Emmanuel has torn down the wall of separation. He will not leave us orphaned and alone. Remember this word the next time you are tempted to ask God, "Where are You?" or "Why is this happening to me?" or "Why didn't You stop that?" Look to the cross for your answer.

"I Thirst"

"After this, Jesus, knowing that all things were now accomplished, that the Scripture might be fulfilled, said, 'I thirst'" (John 19:28). *This word of love speaks of Jesus' own suffering.*

Jesus uttered this word while still in grasp of His faculties. So faithful to the Father's plan was He that He remained "the Word on display" and fulfilled the prophecy spoken by the Spirit through David concerning the last moments of the Messiah's life: "For my thirst they gave me vinegar to drink" (Psalm 69:21).

The One who had turned water to wine could have commanded angels to minister to Him or clouds to pour down their refreshment upon Him. Instead He filled the cup of salvation with His own blood and said, "Let all who are thirsty come and drink." In days past He had asked a Samaritan woman of questionable character for a drink of water in order to give her the water of life. Of this cup He said to His disciples, "Should I not drink it?" He drained it to the dregs for the Father's sake.

It was never about His needs. Reaching the point of no return in the battle and understanding that at last all things had been accomplished, He let His need be known. But even then He allowed His need to be heard only as it did not contradict or hinder the Father's plan.

Particularly in the midst of the storm we must maintain the certainty that God is accomplishing His purpose through our obedient sacrifice. Remember the proverb about prophetic vision: "Where there is no revelation, the people cast off restraint" (Proverbs 29:18). The vision of sons is to complete our mission, no matter how many turn back or who turns against us.

"It Is Finished!"

"So when Jesus had received the sour wine, He said, 'It is finished!'" (John 19:30). *This word of love expresses mission accomplished!*

214

He wet His lips with a drink too late to ease His sufferings so that His voice would ring loud and clear for all creation to hear! The sixth word is the cry of the Victor: Mission accomplished!

That word is a single comprehensive Greek verb, *tetelestai*. It is not the cry of a vanquished victim, but the shout of a victor who has finished the work He came to do. With Scripture fulfilled and having completed all the works He saw the Father doing, only then did He allow Himself—like the marathon runner who breaks the tape—to collapse.

"Father, into Your Hands"

"And when Jesus had cried out with a loud voice, He said, 'Father, "into Your hands I commit My spirit."'" Having said this, He breathed His last" (Luke 23:46; see also Psalm 31:5). *This word of love expresses the joy of the righteous at the end of the day.*

The traditional evening prayer of a pious Jew is made more poignant as we see a beloved Son using His last breath to express His dependence and trust in His Father. His skin flayed, His form marred beyond recognition, there still resides within Him steadfast devotion to the One He came to serve. And so He offered Himself up by the Spirit, their bond of love unbroken till the last.

Too often we see people turn from God and break communion with Him when they are betrayed by those around them. God is the one true Friend and Companion we can always turn to. The Storm Warrior, through the entire ordeal, looked first and last to God for solace and security.

When all is said and done, the righteous one entrusts himself and all that concerns him into the loving grace of his heavenly Father.

In these seven primal utterances made as Jesus poured out His own soul unto death, every part of the human experience is brought to perfect peace through justice. Every argument is silenced. Every question answered. Every accusation muzzled. Every debate settled. Every case resolved.

The Lamb was slain before the foundation of the world. As He offered Himself up by the Spirit to the violent destruction of His body, He brought perfect fulfillment to God's work at the dawn of Creation. There the Spirit of God hovered like a mother eagle stirring up a nest in which to lay her young. The vacuous swirling chaos is called in Hebrew *tohu wa bohu*, "the waste of destruction through judgment." Into that emptiness light erupted as the Word of God was made manifest. At that moment God entered His labor to bring about a new creation. The end of His work was a family of persons made in His own image. The cross of Christ signifies for that family that every victory has been won, every foe vanquished.

Then after three days, in a blinding surge of light, up He came out of hell and death—forever loosed and loosing all who call upon Him!

In all of these words of Jesus we see God's perspective on saint and sinner. We see His obsession with persons and relationship. We see redemptive purpose assigned to trial and even death. We see utter love and utter victory. We see Jesus, the ultimate Storm Warrior.

Overcoming the Last Enemy

As Mahesh mentioned earlier, I, Bonnie, was raised on a cattle ranch in the western United States. My proud heritage comes from the old-time American cowboy, who served as part of the backbone of this country's identity. My grandparents on both sides came West as children, their families homesteading the land and building ranches. My father was part of a disappearing breed of pioneer stock who loved the land and the country that gave them their freedoms as much as they loved life itself. A man of few words with a heart as big as Texas and generosity that knew no bounds, my father was my hero.

A few years ago I woke from a terrible nightmare. I dreamed that a malevolent intruder entered my father's home in the darkness. I was trying to warn my father and stop the thief, but I was unable to do so. A bright flash of gunfire jolted me out of sleep. That dream was literally my worst nightmare. I rebuked it and the devil for trying to torment me, and put the whole thing out of my mind. But a few weeks later the exact dream recurred. This time I could not put it away. A few weeks after that I dreamed it for a third time and knew it was a warning from the Lord.

I talked to my father about it and discovered that indeed someone had threatened him at the rural trading post he kept. When I called to speak with my father early one Saturday and he did not answer his phone, I knew something had happened. The terrible truth became known: My father had been murdered in the night.

What do you do when the worst thing imaginable occurs? How do you respond? Whom do you turn to? Whom do you blame? Where do you go for justice? How do you undo what has been done?

When I received the call that my father was found dead I remember the sense that the Lord was standing in front of me urging me to be careful as to how I responded. He gave me the certain knowledge that my reaction would affect the determinations of the rest of my life.

It reminded me of the time when our first son was struggling for life. Mahesh and I got on our knees and gave Ben and our future over to God. We thanked the Lord for our new son and prayed He would heal him. Then we reaffirmed our devotion to the Lord and His Gospel and said, "No matter what, we will still serve You with all our hearts."

That decision made this one easier. It was one thing to fight an unseen enemy of disease, but the enemy that had broken into our lives and taken my father and my children's grandfather was an evil man. Where was justice? Where was intervention due as a result of the warning in the dream? But there He stood before me as I held the phone in my hand, and in Him was the assurance that my heavenly Father would triumph over all. His was justice to repay. In the meantime the solace of His Spirit would have to suffice as food for our breaking hearts and answer to unanswerable questions.

I flew out West immediately and was in my father's home fewer than 24 hours after his death. The emptiness was palpable. I wanted to reach back across the boundaries of time, lay hold of him in his vibrant life and bring him safely into that empty room where I now stood.

The sight of a small rug, which he used as a table cover, caught my eye. It was lying on the carpet off to one side of the room. I was about to pick it up and replace it but something stopped me. Instead I lifted the edge of the rug with the toe of my shoe. Someone had placed it there to cover the stain of my father's blood spilt on his living room floor.

My eyes rested on the only physical part of him remaining in the place he had lived and loved. Trembling, with tears rolling down my face, I stooped and touched the edge of the bloodstain. My heart seemed to stop. My thoughts were suspended between fear and despair, between faith and disbelief, between shock and revenge. It seemed all sound in the whole of creation went suddenly silent. My father had barely passed his sixtieth birthday, and my children had yet to enjoy their heritage in him as one of the old-time American cowboys. As my trembling hand rested on the crusted dark spot, somewhere from deep within, the cry of my own anguish began to rise. But as it rose louder in my ear, another voice spoke. This was no voice of humans or demons. It sounded like my father's voice—within my Father's voice—speaking out of his blood at my fingertips, saying, *Take no vengeance.*

There is no satisfaction in the absence of justice: The man who committed this heinous act was never apprehended, even though his identity was known. I cannot explain how a balm of calm could settle the cry of anguish in my inner man except that somehow the force of the eternal blood of Christ had mingled in the blood of my father so unjustly shed, and the blood spoke. A sigh of something deeper than resignation escaped my body and set my heart free.

The voice of the blood that flowed down from the cross in the greatest act of injustice seemed to have found its echo in that empty room. The blood that spoke to me that day was crying out better things than the vengeance Abel's blood called for when his own brother took his life in jealous rage. In a place between light and dark, life and death, I knew that my sins had once murdered an innocent Man two thousand years ago. That day in my father's house I was certain the Man spoke for the injustice our family experienced: "'Vengeance is Mine, I will repay,' says the Lord" (Romans 12:19).

As a result of this tragedy in our lives, two generations of our family have been touched with the saving power of the Gospel. That storm created an opportunity for my father's legacy to help some loved ones make course corrections. The ultimate mission of every Christian is victory over the second death. Our message on the journey is that Christ has overcome. Nothing in this life can take away that triumph. Even death in this body holds no threat for the man or woman who has made peace with God through faith in the saving work of Jesus.

In the end we really have no choice but to face the storms that come. We will either overcome them or be overcome by them. I want to repeat something that we stated earlier: Freedom-loving people can grow tired of fighting, but that will not change the fact that there are people who are not at all tired of fighting us. This is especially true in the Church. We can try to pull ourselves out of the storm and sing and have a good time, but the enemy is not taking a break from his path of destruction. He is bent on killing, stealing and destroying everything he can touch. But the breath of this glorious Gospel upon which we have staked our hope fills us with courage. We must gird up our minds in the power of Christ and run toward the battle in courage and faith.

The Firm Foundation

We live in a day and age where every worldview is acceptable but one—the one that has its foundation built on Jesus Christ and His Word. But it is the only foundation that will remain stable for eternity. Without a strong foundation based on faith in Jesus and in God's eternal purpose for us as individuals, families and a nation, we are in danger of losing our moral clarity in the flood of pluralism, humanism, political correctness and terrorism.

Into these raging waters steps the ultimate Storm Warrior. Our view of suffering and death must be reviewed in the surety of His cross. There is no other way to get our bearings in this storm of global chaos. The Church has a call to become relevant to so-called post-modernity. It is time for a reformation proclaiming the true mission of the Gospel.

Jesus said that the Kingdom of heaven is like a man who went on a far journey and said to his servants, "Occupy until I come." This word *occupy* means more than just abide. At this moment councils of war are making demonic plans to murder all who march beneath the banner of the cross of Christ. Our first line of defense is a strong commitment to prayer and the values God has set forth. We have to be willing to pay the price for our liberties. The world is languishing and in need of new storm warriors who will brave this assault and defend our future with their lives.

Jesus taught His disciples that the Kingdom of heaven would advance by violent men moving in the power of the Spirit to heal and deliver those bound by darkness (see Matthew 11:12). The means of advancing the Kingdom of God is described by Paul as wrestling "against principalities, against powers, against the rulers of the darkness of this age, against spiritual hosts of wickedness in the heavenly places" (Ephesians 6:12).

The sign of the cross is the standard that the ultimate Storm Warrior lifted up for all the world to see. It gives witness to good triumphing over evil. It sends a message to a lost and self-obsessed generation that there is hope in the midst of despair. It sends out the pulsating flashes of God's glory and love to all who are perishing in the stormy waves that there was One who was willing to risk His life for others. It assures everyone who looks to His saving strength that there is something worth dying for.

13

COMPLETE THE MISSION

"But you shall receive power when the Holy Spirit has come upon you; and you shall be witnesses to Me in Jerusalem, and in all Judea and Samaria, and to the end of the earth."

Acts 1:8

This is the ultimate mission for every Christian. It has been given to each of us to be an active participant helping to proclaim the Gospel in every nation, with miracles of healing and deliverance attesting to God's power. As the spiritual kingdoms of light and darkness clash in our time, we are called into the fray. The Day of the Lord approaches and the intensity of this storm grows, but so, too, does the release of His power and blessing upon the Church in the earth. Our commitment to the mission and our confidence in Him who commissioned us must grow from glory to glory and from strength to strength. This is the hour of our "watch."

Your gifts and calling are essential. Without your service the whole Body of our glorious Captain is lacking full impact. Let us run toward this battle together in His Spirit.

I, Mahesh, am reminded of a ministry trip to Houston, Texas, where the pastor of a large congregation asked me to release the baptism of the Holy Spirit over the children in his church. Fifty-four children came forward, some of them as young as five and six years old. As I began to pray, I felt a wave of the Spirit release over them, and they instantly began to speak in tongues.

My eyes fell on one young Hispanic boy about five years old. He looked like a little gentleman, dressed in his crisp white shirt and tie, and he started to speak in tongues with an intensity that I have seldom seen in a child. He was crying, the tears streaming down his face, as he began to speak louder in his prayer language. I went to him and tried to comfort him, but he kept weeping and crying out to the Lord until he was shouting as loud as he could in tongues. I continued to minister to the other children and then returned to him. Again, I was not able to quiet him, and he continued to cry out to the Lord.

This lasted for about 25 minutes, until suddenly from the very back of the auditorium, a big Hispanic gentleman ran up weeping and asked to give his life to the Lord. Estranged from his family and seeking a divorce, he did not normally attend church, but he happened to be there that morning. This was the young boy's father. The child did not know that his father was there, but when he was baptized with the Holy Spirit, he entered into the heavenly realm and began to intercede for his father in power and anointing. The boy's prayers brought a breakthrough in the heavenlies and the veil was lifted from his father's eyes. This man came to Christ and was restored to his family before the boy's eyes that night. The intensity of his prayers and faith met the intensity of the need in his family.

Watching the man weeping in repentance while he stood next to his little child who had prayed him into the Kingdom, I was witnessing a fulfillment of Malachi 4:6: "And he will turn the hearts of the fathers to the children, and the hearts of the children to their fathers." This little storm warrior is an example for all of us. In the midst of personal hurt and the breakdown of relationships, the Holy Spirit empowered this young boy to release the power of the Gospel and bring restoration, salvation and healing to his whole family.

Jesus came to a hurting world in order to save, heal and deliver, and He has commissioned every believer to do the same by the power of His Spirit. The enemies of God are on a collision course with His purposes. The central issue of every conflict will be traced back to the mission we carry: "This gospel of the kingdom will be preached in all the world as a witness to all the nations, and then the end will come" (Matthew 24:14). You have been appointed for such a time as this to stand in the storm in the authority and power of our ultimate Storm Warrior, Jesus Christ. You are commissioned as a storm warrior of God.

Mission Possible

American Civil War General William Sherman once said, "The [military commander] must be at the very head of the army—must be seen there, and the effect of his mind and personal energy must be felt by every officer and man." Jesus is the Captain of the Armies of God. He has already triumphed over the ultimate storm on Calvary.

As we go forth to fulfill our mission, we will find that the greater the revelation we have of His love and His authority, the greater will be our ability to stand firm on the day of battle. With each storm we face, the Lord will bring revelation of Himself that will equip and transform us for the victory.

In the book of Revelation, Jesus says, "Do not be afraid; I am the First and the Last. I am He who lives, and was dead, and behold, I am alive forevermore. Amen" (Revelation 1:17–18). He is the One God calls "the faithful witness" (Revelation 1:5). The Greek word translated as "witness" in John's Revelation is a word used throughout the New Testament. It is *martus*, the word from which we get *martyr*. The two words, *witness* and *martyr*, were used interchangeably in the days of the early Church. It is indicative of the Church's attitude. Of the original apostles whom Jesus sent out as His witnesses, all experienced imprisonment, persecution, beatings and abuse during their lifetimes, and almost across the board their witness led to martyrdom for the Kingdom. It was this Revelation of our Captain that the first witnesses needed to stand firm in their mission in the midst of a violent storm.

God can do miracles through even a remnant of those whose hearts are completely set on "mission accomplished." All of us believers are the fruit of the labors of only twelve men who gave their lives to the Captain whom they followed. Within a few hundred years of Christ's ascension, Christianity shaped the foundation of governments across the globe, along with the moral and ethical codes of much of society in general. No longer limited to an obscure sect of religious Jews in Jerusalem, the Christian faith became the foundation of civilization in the Western world.

While we remain in these mortal bodies, battle fatigue is a spiritual sickness resulting from the constant resistance we pose to the kingdom of darkness. Staying freshly anointed by the Holy Spirit day by day is every Christian's prescription for strength, refreshing and healing from the effects of waging spiritual war. Job 29:20 declares, "My glory is fresh within me, and my bow is renewed in my hand." We can receive fresh impartation and empowering of the Holy Spirit to deliver us from the temptation to settle down within the boundaries of anti-Christian pressures that abound and personal setbacks that may come. We will be effective and faithful in our families, in our professions and in our relationships as we allow the Spirit of Christ to fill, refill and glow out through us. He never grows weary and has no limit of supply.

There is an inspiring story from a perilous time in the development of ancient Greece that illustrates beautifully the spirit of storm warriors. During the battle of Theromopylae, "the Hot Gates," Leonidas and his three hundred Spartan warriors faced a Persian invasion in a battle to the last man standing. Theromopylae was a narrow passage that formed the strategic point of entry to the West.

Outnumbered a thousand to one, Leonidas was offered the opportunity to surrender his weapons. His reply? "Come and get them."

They fought for three days. The Spartans' refusal to surrender, together with their willingness to fight to the death, effectively delayed the advance of the Persian invasion. That pause in the Persian advance rallied a loosely knit collection of people called Greece and sparked the raging fire that ultimately repelled and destroyed the Persian army.

The resistance by Leonidas and his men at that critical point resulted in independence for Greece and the development of what is now known as Western civilization.

The heart of the storm warrior is captured in the words of one of those Spartans facing his last battle. Upon hearing that the Persian army was so vast its arrows would blot out the sun, he replied, "All the better. We can fight in the shade."

God has given us a mission and indicated that it will cost us our lives in one manner or another. But He has assured us the greatest victory: eternal salvation of people from every nation. He sends us out in the power of the Holy Spirit with Jesus, the Captain of the Lord's Army, at our head. He is the faithful witness. He has overcome the world and commissions us to do the same.

Shadow of 1938

Writing in his memoirs of the years leading up to the Second World War, Sir Winston Churchill described the night on which he realized the stage was set for Hitler to arise with power of global proportions. The Nazi regime could move largely unhindered because Great Britain, then the greatest military power on the earth, was choosing to stand idly by.

This was February 20, 1938, the only sleepless night that Churchill says he experienced during the war years. "I must confess that my heart sank, and for a while the dark waters of despair overwhelmed me," he wrote. "I watched the daylight creep in through the windows, and saw before me in mental gaze the vision of Death."

Churchill noted that it was not the actions of the enemy that "consumed him with emotions of sorrow and fear." It was the resignation of Foreign Secretary Anthony Eden, the last man in the British Cabinet who was not afraid to stand and face the enemy's threats. The British Empire was now in the hands of those who would give the enemy victory without a fight. She had crossed the point of no return into another worldwide conflict because of her unwillingness to resist her enemy.

Britain and her Allies from the previous "Great War" were weary and reluctant to endure the hardship and cost of another large-scale confrontation. Appeasement was the reigning policy of that day. While Hitler amassed troops and made steps to annex neighboring countries, British Prime Minister Neville Chamberlain signed resolutions with him and spoke to the British people and Parliament of "peace in our time." Churchill and a few others were the lone voices who recognized that there is no peace without readiness for war. As Chamberlain tossed Czechoslovakia to the Nazi wolves and declared diplomatic victory, Churchill responded before Parliament:

> We have suffered a total and unmitigated defeat . . . the consequences of which will travel far with us along our road . . . we have passed an awful milestone in our history, when . . . the terrible words have for the time being been pronounced against the Western democracies: "Thou art weighed in the balance and found wanting." And do not suppose that this is the end. This is only the beginning of the reckoning. This is only the first sip, the first foretaste of a bitter cup which will be proffered to us year by year unless by a supreme recovery of moral health and martial vigour, we arise again and take our stand for freedom as in the olden time.

Churchill's speech was interrupted repeatedly by angry shouts from his fellow House of Commons members: "We want peace! We want peace!" But Churchill's understanding of the times was correct, and it was not many years hence that Britain was pulled into a battle she was ill-prepared to fight.

These are no longer only dreadful specters of past history. The world, the Church, Western civilization and the fate of future generations are all poised in similar circumstances. Like Churchill, we stand in the shadows before a dawning clash of kingdoms. In the growing light we will see more and more clearly a spiritual battle made manifest in the kingdoms of the earth. The forces of spiritual wickedness in high places are amassing the ranks of their last stand against Christ and His anointed ones. Nations that spew threats toward Israel and countries built on Judeo-Christian values are gaining in ascendancy. Many would like to compromise with the enemy, hoping to avoid war within their own borders. But there is no peace without war. There can be no compromise if our children are to live in liberty and blessing.

Where do we start? We must have a supernatural army advancing before the natural elements of this clash of kingdoms. When Jesus saw the final storm brewing on His horizon, He went to the Garden of Gethsemane. He showed us that the path to victory begins in the crucible of prayer.

This is our most powerful supernatural weapon. The consistent, persistent petitions of the man or woman walking in harmony with God in the fellowship of His Holy Spirit will be answered. God is leading His warrior Bride into corporate spiritual combat through prayer and fasting as never before in her history. Every believer is officially on active duty status.

Prayer is made effective as the spiritual storm warriors of Christ who know Him intimately take an uncompromising

stand for God's agenda. Victory will be costly. It will require putting courageous faith-filled feet to the prayers we
pray.

Jesus likened the last days, the days we are in, to the days
of Lot and Noah. Moral confusion and social violence are
rampant in every culture. Political correctness and intellectual pride have married the spirit of compromise and
have caused many to relinquish godly values. False religions
threaten the foundations of past generations laid down
through the influence of the Gospel. In traditionally Christian nations, children are forbidden to wear emblems of the
cross to school. Christmas carols that sing of Jesus as a baby
are banned in public establishments. Store owners prevent
their employees from wishing customers "Merry Christmas." Prayer to Christ is not allowed in public schools. At
the same time, sexual experimentation and perversion is
flaunted and celebrated in textbooks. The terms *natural
marriage* and *family values* were ruled by a U.S. circuit
court to be "hate speech" and ordered removed from a
company office bulletin board. In Britain, references to
Winston Churchill are being removed from high school
history classes because he offends immigrant sensibilities.
Judeo-Christian ideology, prosperity and liberty hang in
the balance.

The power behind these philosophies is not merely
human. The ultimate power behind moral corruption and
philosophical and religious confusion and darkness is spiritual. Christ broke the dominion of these powers and openly
displayed their secrets on Calvary. The battle being waged
on this earth has been fought and won in the heavens, but
the aftermath is apparent in our time. The fate of the world
is in the hands of Christians in this present hour.

Raise Up a Generation

The Old Testament story of King Hezekiah holds many lessons for the modern-day storm warrior. Hezekiah was a contradiction in values. When he came to the throne, he demolished Israel's connection with idolatry. As king, however, Hezekiah remained naïve in his diplomatic ties with the kingdoms bent on conquering Israel. While he built strategic defenses to enable Jerusalem to survive against any natural siege, he continued to be impressed with powerful world leaders who came to call and made alliances with those who sought to conquer him. Repeatedly Hezekiah toured them around his city and showed them everything he owned. It seems he truly believed that because he had only right intentions toward them, they intended only good in return. Though his personal faith was firmly intact, he exercised little wisdom in dealing with the greater strategic spiritual threat facing his nation.

At the time, seven hundred years before Christ, Assyria was the world superpower and was bent on the conquest of the entire world, including the destruction of Israel. Assyrian King Sennacherib had set his sights on Egypt and his campaign led him straight through Jerusalem. Hezekiah found his nation in the crosshairs of destruction:

"Say now to Hezekiah, 'Thus says the great king, the king of Assyria: "What confidence is this in which you trust? I say you speak of having plans and power for war; but they are mere words. Now in whom do you trust, that you rebel against me? Look! You are trusting in the staff of this broken reed, Egypt, on which if a man leans, it will go into his hand and pierce it. . . . "' Now therefore, I urge you, give a pledge to my master the king of Assyria, and I will give you two thousand horses—if you are able on your part to put riders on them!". . .

Then the Rabshakeh stood and called out with a loud voice in Hebrew, and said, "Hear the words of the great king, the king of Assyria! Thus says the king: 'Do not let Hezekiah deceive you, for he will not be able to deliver you; nor let Hezekiah make you trust in the LORD, saying, "The LORD will surely deliver us; this city will not be given into the hand of the king of Assyria."' Do not listen to Hezekiah; for thus says the king of Assyria: 'Make peace with me by a present and come out to me; and every one of you eat from his own vine and every one from his own fig tree, and every one of you drink the waters of his own cistern; until I come and take you away to a land like your own land. . . . Where are the gods of Hamath and Arpad? Where are the gods of Sepharvaim? Indeed, have they delivered Samaria from my hand? Who among all the gods of these lands have delivered their countries from my hand, that the LORD should deliver Jerusalem from my hand?'". . .

And so it was, when King Hezekiah heard it, that he tore his clothes, covered himself with sackcloth, and went into the house of the LORD. . . . "Thus says Hezekiah: 'This day is a day of trouble and rebuke and blasphemy; for the children have come to birth, but there is no strength to bring them forth.'"

Isaiah 36:4–6, 8, 13–17, 19–20; 37:1, 3

As the Assyrian ambassador for war, the Rabshakeh had already conquered several cities in Judah. Sennacherib was confident that those victories would frighten Hezekiah into surrender, without the pain of a drawn-out siege. The Rabshakeh delivered his message directly to the people in their own language, terrorizing them in an attempt to force King Hezekiah to comply. How similar to current world affairs with the spirits of antichrist, secular humanism, jihadism and anti-Semitism pouring out upon the earth today! Once again Jerusalem and Israel are in the crosshairs of God's enemies. And with her are the Church and the future of Western civilization.

The Assyrian enemies of Israel offered a semblance of life as usual in exchange for surrender. We see shadows of this as the Church is being lured into tolerance for standards that our Bible clearly rejects. But acceptance of these vile philosophies will not be enough to satisfy the spirit insisting on tolerance. Once we accept these non-values we will be forced to celebrate and teach them to our children. We must be clear and courageous and hold out the simple word of truth that salvation is found only in repentance before God and through the blood of Christ. The threats of the Rabshakeh were a powerful blow to the will of God's people. From Hezekiah's response to the threat, we learn several important principles for lasting victory in the battles we face.

1. Humble Yourself before God

And so it was, when King Hezekiah heard it, that he tore his clothes, covered himself with sackcloth, and went into the house of the LORD.

Isaiah 37:1

Hezekiah's first response to the threat of the enemy was not to get angry, defend his mistakes, build an army or take an opinion poll. It was to humble himself before God. Poor decisions he had made earlier had backfired.

God gives grace to the humble. As we submit our lives and wills to Jesus, His blood cleanses and we can be restored.

Hezekiah knew that the only place for deliverance was at the mercy seat of God-of-the-Angel-Armies.

2. Seek the Anointed Word of the Lord

Then he sent Eliakim, who was over the household, Shebna the scribe, and the elders of the priests, covered with sackcloth, to Isaiah the prophet, the son of Amoz.

Isaiah 37:2

God has a living Word for everyone who runs to Him in sincerity. We receive "grace to help in time of need" (Hebrews 4:16). The anointed Word may be instruction, direction or correction, but always the anointing breaks the yoke (see Isaiah 10:27). Though Hezekiah was the king, he summoned the servant of the Lord for light and direction. Isaiah answered with the Word of the Lord.

3. Do Not Fear the Enemy

And Isaiah said to them, . . . "Thus says the LORD: 'Do not be afraid of the words which you have heard, with which the servants of the king of Assyria have blasphemed Me. Surely I will send a spirit upon him, and he shall hear a rumor and return to his own land; and I will cause him to fall by the sword in his own land.'"

Isaiah 37:6–7

Satan is a master at creating fear. It is his most powerful tool. He uses it to paralyze his victims. The present global rise of terrorism is based on fear. But, as we noted earlier, Scripture tells us that "God has not given us a spirit of fear, but of power and of love and of a sound mind" (2 Timothy 1:7). Also,

There is no fear in love [dread does not exist], but full-grown (complete, perfect) love turns fear out of doors and expels every trace of terror! For fear brings with it the thought of punishment, and [so] he who is afraid has not reached the full maturity of love [is not yet grown into love's complete perfection].

1 John 4:18, AMP

When we have Christ there is nothing the enemy can bring against us that we need to be afraid of. It is essential that we have a living revelation in our lives of Christ as perfect love. We develop this as we learn to dwell in His presence.

In the Old Testament God's manifest presence or glory is the *shekinah*. It is the secret place where we can hide; it is the "shadow of the Almighty" spoken of in Psalm 91:1. The psalmist says,

You shall not be afraid of the terror by night, nor of the arrow that flies by day, nor of the pestilence that walks in darkness, nor of the destruction that lays waste at noonday.... Because he has set his love upon Me, therefore I will deliver him.

verses 5–6, 14

God is not the source of dark fears. If the enemy has tried to intimidate us and hold us captive in certain areas, we can take authority over the spirit of fear, renounce it and cast it out of our hearts and our homes. As intercessors, we can even cast it away from our nation. The stronghold of fear can be shattered through Christ's authority.

Those who choose cowardice and fear have no place in the ranks of God's spiritual army. He sent them home in Gideon's day and He cannot use them in battle today. Fear leads to compromise. Compromise with the devil is high treason in the battle between good and evil. Notice that the opposite of courage is not fear; it is discouragement. In the days of Nehemiah, when the enemies of Israel tried to halt the work of rebuilding the city walls, he spoke these words: "Do not be afraid of [the enemy]. Remember the Lord, great and awesome, and fight for your brethren, your sons, your daughters, your wives, and your houses" (Nehemiah 4:14).

4. Never Give In

And Hezekiah received the letter from the hand of the messengers, and read it; and Hezekiah went up to the house of the Lord, and spread it before the Lord.

Isaiah 37:14

Perseverance is vital in spiritual battle. The tactic of the devil is to wear down the saints. If he can run you around long enough, you may give in to defeat. Sennacherib sent Hezekiah a letter repeating his threat. Hezekiah did not lose heart or let go of Isaiah's prophecy. Hezekiah held before the Lord the very blasphemies that God had said He would avenge in Isaiah's prophecy. He took his battle to the Lord and let the anointed Word direct his prayers. His prayer was effective because it lined up with the heart and Word of the Lord. God responded and sent His angel to rout the enemy armies.

Winston Churchill was often quoted for his admiration of the British bulldog: "The nose of the bulldog is slanted backward so it can continue to breathe without letting go," he said. And famous words of his, part of a speech given to a class at Harrow School in October 1941, still stir hearts: "Never give in. Never give in. Never, never, never, never—in nothing, great or small, large or petty—never give in, except to convictions of honor and good sense. Never yield to force. Never yield to the apparently overwhelming might of the enemy."

Storm warriors have in them the power of persistence never to quit. Perseverance becomes a lifestyle for the storm warrior. Recall this verse we quoted in chapter 3: "Therefore we also, since we are surrounded by so great a cloud of witnesses, let us lay aside every weight, and the sin which so easily ensnares us, and let us run with endurance the race that is set before us" (Hebrews 12:1).

Endurance, along with faithful attendance to daily disciplines, adds up to perseverance for great spiritual tasks. Our consistent exercise of faith and discipline in prayer, fasting, service, study in the Word of God and commitment to the mission is our worship. It gives us the strength we need to help others steer through crises. Those who persevere will be like Elijah when he received the report that a cloud was signaling the end of drought. He girded up his loins and outran horses and chariot.

5. Magnify the Lord

Then Hezekiah prayed to the LORD, saying: "O LORD of hosts, God of Israel, the One who dwells between the cherubim, You are God, You alone, of all the kingdoms of the earth. You have made heaven and earth. Incline Your ear, O LORD, and hear; open Your eyes, O LORD, and see; and hear all the words of Sennacherib, which he has sent to reproach the living God. . . . Now therefore, O LORD our God, save us from his hand, that all the kingdoms of the earth may know that You are the LORD, You alone."

Isaiah 37:15–17, 20

Make God *big* through praise. The key words of Hezekiah's prayers, when all was said and done, are two: *You alone.* Those who know their God will do exploits. Salvation is in no other. "And whatever you ask in My name, that I will do, that the Father may be glorified in the Son" (John 14:13).

We have learned over the years to keep the Lord mighty in our hearts. We enter battle in the spirit of praise. Whatever our battle, God is bigger. This was the key that, for David, turned battle after battle into victory after victory. Psalm 34:1, 3–4 reveals his heart: "I will bless the LORD at all times; His praise shall continually be in my mouth. . . . Oh, magnify the LORD with me, and let us exalt His name together. I sought the LORD, and He heard me, and delivered me from all my fears."

In the middle of a storm we clear our hearts of anxiety and worry and make room for His glory by magnifying the Lord. Psalm 24:7–8, 10, says, "Lift up your heads, O you gates! And be lifted up, you everlasting doors! And the King of glory shall come in. Who is this King of glory? The LORD strong and mighty, the LORD mighty in battle. . . . He is the King of glory." When you are confronting the enemy in battle, do not focus on or magnify the enemy. Magnify the King of glory and let Him invade your situation.

6. Expect the Breakthrough

Then Isaiah the son of Amoz sent to Hezekiah, saying, "Thus says the LORD God of Israel: 'Because you have prayed to Me against Sennacherib king of Assyria, I have heard.'"

2 Kings 19:20

Hezekiah's heart was full of faith and hope, and he received this word from a proven servant of God. It is essential that hope fill our hearts in the midst of the battle. Hope is the essential abiding grace of our faith. The one who relinquishes hope in God will also lose faith and give up love for God. Biblical hope is not "pie-in-the-sky," "up one day and down the next" depending on the circumstances. Our hope is real. Christian hope is an anchor in every storm, because it is the firm confidence that Christ has triumphed over every enemy—including death. We possess the knowledge that the tyrants of this present darkness shall ultimately bow to the name above all names. And so we rejoice now in hope, knowing that Jesus is Lord of heaven and earth.

7. Learn from Past Mistakes

At that time Berodach-Baladan the son of Baladan, king of Babylon, sent letters and a present to Hezekiah, for he heard that Hezekiah had been sick. And Hezekiah was attentive to them, and showed them all the house of his treasures—the silver and gold, the spices and precious ointment, and all his armory—all that was found among his treasures. There was nothing in his house or in all his dominion that Hezekiah did not show them.

2 Kings 20:12–13

Those who refuse to learn from their history will repeat their worst moments. One of Hezekiah's tendencies was that he did not seem to learn from his past mistakes. Once a crisis passed, his wealth and prosperity would lure him into a false sense of security and his enemies would catch him off balance once again. The peace and prosperity enjoyed for a while in the wake of the Lord's deliverance would be lost as Hezekiah fell for flattery and opened the door to invasion. The devil does not invent new strategies if you will fall for the same old ones. If you leave a hole in the wall of your defenses, especially if you have made those mistakes in the past, be certain the devil will find it and come through again.

8. *Keep Your Priorities Straight*

For he said, "Will there not be peace and truth at least in my days?"

2 Kings 20:19

The deceitfulness of riches was not the king's only weakness. He had a much more serious character flaw. Although Hezekiah is mentioned as the "most righteous" king in Israel's history, one who feared the Lord and restored worship to God, his legacy is marred by his failure to raise up a righteous generation after him. He built strategic natural defenses and innovations by which Jerusalem could survive under siege—his water tunnel is still in existence today. But those defenses could not hold against the spiritual enemies welcomed by the son who became king after him. Manasseh led Judah into idolatry and is considered "the most wicked" of all Israel's rulers. Manasseh's wickedness sent the nation into exile.

The basic building block of a society is the family. We must build today with the generation of tomorrow in mind. More than teaching a child how to succeed or giving him a good education or even finding him a good mate, the first priority of parents is to train up a child in the ways of the Lord: "Train up a child in the way he should go, and when he is old he will not depart from it" (Proverbs 22:6). Hezekiah fell into the trap of being caught up in his own survival and success. He was willing to settle for peace in his own day, regardless of what that meant for future generations.

241

The point is vital for our lasting and ultimate victory in the storms we face. We must teach our sons and daughters to fear the Lord. We must train them to walk in a lasting heritage that no passage of time and no enemy can take away.

The prophet Isaiah tells the story of Hezekiah. His words give us the next lesson from the king's history.

9. Lay Hold of Lasting Victory

Then the angel of the LORD went out, and killed in the camp of the Assyrians one hundred and eighty-five thousand; and when people arose early in the morning, there were the corpses—all dead. So Sennacherib king of Assyria departed and went away, returned home, and remained at Nineveh.

Isaiah 37:36–37

It seems impossible that such a victory could ever be mishandled, but Hezekiah was repeatedly naïve concerning his enemies. That naiveté made trouble for Israel over and over again. At one point he thought he could use his wealth to buy off the Assyrians. That mistake gave the oppressor the foothold from which only supernatural intervention could bring deliverance.

There are many instances our own generation faces that threaten annihilation except that God intervenes. Believers are the key to that deliverance. If we slip into the slumber of humanistic thinking and relinquish a biblical worldview, we and our children will be swallowed alive by the enemy's devices. In our own country, the Judeo-Christian foundations upon which we have stood for two centuries are being shaken by the enemies of our faith. The prosperity those foundations have proffered us is not guaranteed without a fight. We must make provision for the victory in our own and in our children's generations. If we lay hold of our spiritual destiny and of our God in truth, we can rout the enemy encampments already laid in siege against us. God-of-the-Angel-Armies is ready to battle on our behalf.

Hezekiah led his nation into a season of revival—cleansing the land of idolatry and turning the people back to God—but lasting and effective revival must be generational. The true spiritual state of his nation was revealed in his message to Isaiah: "This day is a day of trouble and rebuke and blasphemy; for the children have come to birth, but there is no strength to bring them forth" (Isaiah 37:3).

Revival is the outpouring of the rains of the Spirit on dry ground, bringing to life seed-bearing fruit for the next generation. It is costly. It will involve sacrifice to sustain it. Otherwise, a season of refreshing without attention to the next generation is little more than personal and temporary comfort. Hezekiah's willingness to compromise his nation's inheritance for a life of ease was the real enemy. Ultimately, it caused her downfall.

Our inheritance is in our children. Our lives count not only for ourselves, but also as an investment in the generations coming after us. Christ laid down His life that He might bring many sons to glory. When our lives are laid down in Christ as an offering to the Lord, there is supernatural strength to bring forth righteousness in the children coming after us.

For Such a Time as This

American general George Patton demonstrated tenacity that facilitated some of the greatest Allied victories of World War II. His indomitable force against all enemies boosted the morale of those he commanded. As they marched out to war he told them, "Men, one day when your grandbaby climbs into your lap and looks up at you and asks, 'Granddaddy, what did you do in the Great War?' you will not have to hang your head in shame and say, 'I was shoveling manure in Louisiana.' You will be able to look him in the eye and say, 'Honey, I was right in the midst of the battle when the nations of the world were hanging in the balance!'"

Even as He foretold through the prophets of old, God's own great outpouring of the Holy Spirit upon all flesh will soon fill the earth with His glory and destroy the works of evil in His path. God is preparing His Church and gathering up His mighty men and women for war. He is amassing His troops in the face of an unprecedented satanic assault. Every spiritual storm has the potential to help usher in His glory. But God's great army must develop perseverance, tenacity and patience if we are to endure the warfare that is taking place. Above all, we must not pull back, cut back or turn back until we have destroyed the works of the enemy.

The onslaught of the enemy should not wear us out. We can use the intensity to help us grow stronger and freer in the truth of our salvation. We can turn adversity into a vehicle to serve our spiritual purposes. As we receive the Lord's strength, we ride the storm to our destinies.

We will begin to see more and more clearly in these last days that the flood coming from the serpent's mouth is directed specifically at two targets: Christianity and the nation of Israel. The dark alliance sees Israel's Messiah and those who follow Him as a threat to their kingdoms. The battle may be new, but the war is an ancient one fought by those who resist faith in the God of the Bible. The one true Friend to man is slandered by the deceiver of the world as being mankind's greatest threat.

God told Moses, "Lift up your rod, and stretch out your hand over the sea and divide it. And the children of Israel shall go on dry ground through the midst of the sea" (Exodus 14:16). Moses had been equipped for the battle when God first called him. The glory of God at the burning bush had transformed Moses—and his staff. He exercised his faith that God would deliver Israel by using the rod to release supernatural authority.

In this same manner the Holy Spirit transforms us through faith in Jesus Christ, equipping us with supernatural authority and the weapons of our warfare. Our weapons are anointed with newly realized effectiveness and accuracy. These are the name of Jesus, the blood of Jesus and the Word of God. It is when we exercise faith in God and in His Word and wield those weapons that we are able to gain the victory.

> Let this mind be in you which was also in Christ Jesus, who, being in the form of God, did not consider it robbery to be equal with God, but made Himself of no reputation, taking the form of a bondservant, and coming in the likeness of men. And being found in appearance as a man, He humbled Himself and became obedient to the point of death, even the death of the cross. Therefore God also has highly exalted Him and given Him the name which is above every name, that at the name of Jesus every knee should bow, of those in heaven, and of those on earth, and of those under the earth, and that every tongue should confess that Jesus Christ is Lord, to the glory of God the Father.
>
> Philippians 2:5–11

We are surrounded by a great cloud of witnesses, storm warriors who have gone before us in obedience to our Captain, laying down life and limb in confidence that, though they did not see the promise in their day, each succeeding generation would bring it closer to fulfillment. This is the heritage we have received.

Your faithfulness is the hallmark of character in God's eyes. As storm warriors of the Kingdom of light we are to take the high ground of this world through faith and occupy it until He comes. Kingdoms will rise to oppose us, but whether we are confronting enemies abroad or at home we will use every weapon in our arsenal to do the job. Individuals and whole nations are being held captive by elite forces of spiritual wickedness. We assault them from the air with praise, prayer and fasting, and then move in on the ground with apostolic teams equipped to set the captives free.

We are God's end time army. We have received a mission and the authority to complete it:

"All authority has been given to Me in heaven and on earth. Go therefore and make disciples of all the nations, baptizing them in the name of the Father and of the Son and of the Holy Spirit, teaching them to observe all things that I have commanded you; and lo, I am with you always, even to the end of the age."

Matthew 28:18-20

Spiritual vision that ignites the life of a disciple is the secret for a fully successful life in Christ. While salvation is a "free" gift that no man can earn by his works, faith without those works is dead. We are debtors, then, to live for Christ as a testimony that His death and resurrection are relevant for every human being alive today.

Canon Andrew White, personal representative of the archbishop of Canterbury, present vicar of Baghdad, blessed us not too long ago with a gift in honor of our ministry's help in caring for widows and orphans in Iraq. The gift was a military patch worn by Coalition troops fighting to give many in the Middle East an opportunity for life and liberty. The patch carries the slogan "Honor the dead, complete the mission."

There are times when words fail. In those instances we look at those who have lived their lives in such a way as to be etched in the annals of time. Their testimonies echo down through human history, leaving a mark to which successive generations strive. We see such heroes in every age of the Christian faith. So many of them are the great men and women of old from whom we gain fresh determination in a new generation. They laid down their lives for the Master and for us. We cannot cease to strive to make the heritage they left us fruitful. We owe a debt to them. And we have something to add to that faith.

Our decisions are pivotal. We were never guaranteed life without conflict. We cannot be naïve about the battle we are in or about the strategies of the enemies we face. We must make provision for the victory in our own and in our children's generations.

We have been appointed as storm warriors for such a time as this. There is One who was dead for our sakes and who is yet alive. He speaks to us today. His blood sprinkled a battlefield between heaven and earth and conquered every foe in heaven, on earth and under the earth. His death means life for everyone who believes. His life lives on in everyone who receives Him. That life in us brings forth the same power that brought Him out of the grave. He is with us in power. This, then, would be our final word to every storm warrior: Honor the One who died and is alive forever more. And complete the mission.

NOTES

1. Brian Greene, quoted in "The Elegant Universe: String's the Thing," transcript, *NOVA*, October 28, 2003, http://www.pbs.org/wgbh/nova/transcripts/3013_elegant.html.

2. Ernest Shackleton, *South: The Endurance Expedition* (New York: Signet, 1999), 230.

3. Ian Corkett, "Piercing the Veneer of Outside Things," Aiglon College, January 25, 2002, http://www.aiglon.ch/archive/meds/ic1.shtm.

4. John Rabe, "Walking Out of History: The True Story of Shackleton's Endurance Expedition," American RadioWorks, October 1999, http://americanradioworks.publicradio.org/features/walking/part06/index.html.

Mahesh Chavda, Ph.D., D.Min., and **Bonnie Chavda**, D.Min., have served together in full-time ministry for more than thirty years, reaching the nations with the Gospel accompanied by signs and wonders. Hundreds of thousands of people have come to salvation, and thousands have received healing from critical diseases like AIDS and cancer through their ministry. Many of these miracles have been documented, including healings of stage IV cancer, lameness, deafness and blindness and the resurrection from the dead of a six-year-old boy.

Through *The Watch* television program produced by Mahesh Chavda Ministries, Mahesh and Bonnie reach a potential audience of one billion households every week with the saving message of Jesus and are equipping believers to walk in the power and anointing of the Holy Spirit. They are touching people across the globe through satellite broadcast, including the Middle East, where they are deeply impacting the region through Arabic and Farsi translations of their program. In addition, Mahesh and Bonnie have produced many useful tools for believers, including their books *Only Love Can Make a Miracle, The Hidden Power of Prayer and Fasting, The Hidden Power of Healing Prayer* and *The Hidden Power of a Woman*.

Together the Chavdas pastor All Nations Church and Healing Center in Charlotte, North Carolina, and spearhead a global prayer movement, The Watch of the Lord, where they have been leading their congregation in weekly corporate prayer for more than a decade.

For more information contact:

Mahesh Chavda Ministries
All Nations Church
The Watch television program
P.O. Box 411008
Charlotte, NC 28241

Phone: 1-800-730-6264
Fax: (704) 541-5300

E-mail: info@maheshchavda.com
Website: http://maheshchavda.com